AMERICAN POLITICAL, ECONOMIC, AND SECURITY ISSUES

U. S. SAVINGS BONDS, MUNICIPAL BONDS AND TAX-EXEMPT BONDS

SELECTED ANALYSES AND ISSUES

American Political, Economic, and Security Issues

Additional books in this series can be found on Nova's website under the Series tab.

Additional e-books in this series can be found on Nova's website under the e-book tab.

AMERICAN POLITICAL, ECONOMIC, AND SECURITY ISSUES

U.S. SAVINGS BONDS, MUNICIPAL BONDS AND TAX-EXEMPT BONDS

SELECTED ANALYSES AND ISSUES

HENRIETTA WALTERS
EDITOR

nova publishers
New York

Library of Congress Cataloging-in-Publication Data

ISBN: 978-1-63484-698-1

Published by Nova Science Publishers, Inc. † New York

CONTENTS

PREFACE

U.S. savings bonds provide Americans with an affordable way to save. In 2012, Treasury stopped selling paper savings bonds at banks as part of its broader electronic initiative. As a result, savings bonds generally must be purchased through TreasuryDirect®. The one exception is the Tax Time Savings Bond program, established in 2010 to enable taxpayers to use their tax refund to buy paper savings bonds. The program is one way for lower-income families to save. Chapter One of this book examines the effect of Treasury's elimination of paper U.S. savings bonds on the program and bond purchases; the extent to which the Tax Time Savings Bond program has promoted savings by lower-income households and Treasury's future plans for the program; and the extent to which lower-income households are saving and programs developed by federal agencies and others. Chapter Two informs Congress about various developments related to the demand for municipal bonds, which are debt securities issued by states, cities, counties, and other government-created agencies to finance capital projects, such as highways, airports, sewers, bridges, schools, hospitals, and other public goods for residents. Chapter Three provides information about state and local government debt.

In: U.S. Savings Bonds, Municipal Bonds … ISBN: 978-1-63484-698-1
Editor: Henrietta Walters

Chapter 1

U.S. SAVINGS BONDS: FUTURE OF OFFERING PAPER SAVINGS BONDS AT TAX TIME IS UNCERTAIN, AND LOWER-INCOME HOUSEHOLDS CONTINUE TO FACE SAVINGS CHALLENGES*

United States Government Accountability Office

ABBREVIATIONS

FDIC	Federal Deposit Insurance Corporation
FLEC	Financial Literacy and Education Commission
HUD	Department of Housing and Urban Development
IRS	Internal Revenue Service
SCF	Survey of Consumer Finances
Treasury	Department of the Treasury
TRIM	Treasury Retail Investment Manager

* This is an edited, reformatted and augmented version of The United States Government Accountability Office publication, GAO-15-563, dated July 2015.

Why GAO Did This Study

U.S. savings bonds provide Americans with an affordable way to save. In 2012, Treasury stopped selling paper savings bonds at banks as part of its broader electronic initiative. As a result, savings bonds generally must be purchased through TreasuryDirect®. The one exception is the Tax Time Savings Bond program, established in 2010 to enable taxpayers to use their tax refund to buy paper savings bonds. The program is one way for lower-income families to save.

You requested that GAO examine Treasury's savings bond program, including the accessibility of TreasuryDirect, and other savings programs. This report examines (1) the effect of Treasury's elimination of paper U.S. savings bonds on the program and bond purchases, (2) the extent to which the Tax Time Savings Bond program has promoted savings by lower-income households and Treasury's future plans for the program, and (3) the extent to which lower-income households are saving and programs developed by federal agencies and others. GAO reviewed agency rules and other documents; analyzed Treasury, Internal Revenue Service, and other data, in part using economic models; and interviewed federal, state, and nonprofit entities and experts involved in savings programs.

What GAO Recommends

GAO recommends that as Treasury implements the TRIM system, it consider the benefits and costs of the Tax Time program in future decisions on whether to extend the program. Treasury agreed with GAO's recommendation.

What GAO Found

The Department of the Treasury's (Treasury) elimination of paper savings bonds made buying bonds more difficult for some customers, but GAO's analyses generally indicated that the decline in bond purchases after the change was not statistically significant. Treasury eliminated paper savings bonds in January 2012, after a long-term decline in savings bond purchases. It estimated the change would save about $70 million in program costs from 2012 through 2016. Except for the Tax Time Savings Bond program, customers who want to buy savings bonds must use TreasuryDirect—an online system that requires users to have Internet access and a bank account. Customers without both, which likely includes lower-income households, face challenges accessing TreasuryDirect. Treasury is in the early stages of developing a new system, the Treasury Retail Investment Manager (TRIM), to make it easier to buy savings bonds, such as by using a mobile device, which often is the primary means of accessing the Internet for many lower-income households.

A little more than one-third of the users of Treasury's Tax Time Savings Bond program—the only way to purchase paper bonds—were lower-income tax filers (filers with an adjusted gross income of $25,000 or less), but the program's future is uncertain. Since 2010, tax filers have been able to use a tax form to buy paper savings bonds with their tax refund. For tax years 2010 through 2013, about 142,000 tax filers (less than 1 percent of tax filers receiving refunds) used at least part of their tax refund to buy nearly $72.5 million in savings bonds. Of these filers, about 55,000 had incomes of $25,000 or less and bought about $13.7 million in savings bonds, or about $250, on average, per filer each year. Treasury has been extending the program partly because the amount of bonds purchased and participation levels indicate that the program is providing benefits, but it generally has not considered the program's costs. In May 2015, Treasury officials told GAO that they plan to continue to extend the program until TRIM can provide a suitable electronic alternative. Because TRIM will require Internet access by computer or mobile device, Tax Time program users without such access may no longer be able to save by buying bonds with their refunds after TRIM is implemented. In prior work on agency stewardship of public funds, GAO reported that agencies, as a best practice, should consider both benefits and costs in considering alternatives related to program decisions. Without considering both, Treasury cannot make a fully informed decision on whether to discontinue the Tax Time program when an electronic alternative is available.

On the basis of GAO's analysis of data from the most recent Survey of Consumer Finances conducted in 2013, the median value of financial assets held by the bottom fifth of income earners (whose median annual income was $14,200) was $550. Given the limited savings of lower-income households and savings challenges faced by such households, a number of federal agencies have developed programs to promote savings. For example, Treasury's *my*RA®, which is in a soft-launch phase, promotes retirement savings for individuals without access to employer-sponsored retirement plans. State, local, and nonprofit agencies also have initiated programs that promote savings for retirement, child development, or emergencies and generally target lower-income households. Eligibility requirements and participation vary by program.

* * *

July 16, 2015

Congressional Requesters

In 2013, Treasury issued about $686 million in U.S. savings bonds, which historically have provided Americans with an affordable and safe way to save and invest. However, fewer than 5 percent of lower-income households owned savings bonds that same year. Additionally, savings bond purchases have declined significantly from 2001 to 2013. Savings bonds are low risk, backed by the full faith and credit of the U.S. government, and offered in minimum denominations as low as $25. Beginning in January 2012, the U.S. Department of the Treasury (Treasury) discontinued the over-the-counter sale of paper savings bonds at financial institutions as part of its agency-wide, all-electronic effort announced in 2010. As a result, savings bonds generally can be purchased only through Treasury's Internet-based system, called TreasuryDirect®. Treasury stated that its goal in discontinuing sales of paper savings bonds was to reduce costs and enhance customer service by increasing electronic transactions. At the same time, some members of Congress, nonprofit organizations, and others have raised concerns that the change has reduced access to an important savings product, particularly for lower-income households who may not have bank accounts, access to the Internet, or the knowledge or skills needed to use TreasuryDirect. In 2010, the Internal Revenue Service (IRS) provided tax filers with an alternative method for purchasing paper savings bonds by enabling them to use their income tax refund to buy them through a program commonly known as the Tax Time Savings Bond program. This program is intended, in part, to help lower-income households to save. In addition to this program, federal agencies, state agencies, and nonprofit organizations have developed an array of savings or asset-building programs, many of which target lower-income households.

You asked us to review issues related to Treasury's savings bond program and study other programs that promote savings by lower-income households. This report examines (1) the effect of Treasury's elimination of paper U.S. savings bonds, including on the savings bond program and bond purchases; (2)

the extent to which Treasury's Tax Time Savings Bond program has promoted savings, particularly by lower-income households, and Treasury's plans for the program's future; and (3) the extent to which lower-income households are saving using financial products, and some of the government and nonprofit programs that have been developed to promote savings by lower-income households.

To examine the effect of Treasury's elimination of paper U.S. savings bonds, including on the savings bond program and bond purchases, we analyzed Treasury's data on savings bond purchases from 2001 through 2013. Specifically, to analyze long-term trends in savings bond purchases and more recent trends since the end of paper sales in January 2012, we estimated two econometric models. We also reviewed Treasury documentation, including estimates of cost savings from eliminating paper savings bonds, budgets and capital investment plans, and TreasuryDirect materials. We interviewed Treasury officials to discuss its savings bond program, including the benefits and costs of eliminating paper savings bonds, concerns that had been raised about TreasuryDirect, and plans for replacing TreasuryDirect.

To determine the extent to which Treasury's Tax Time Savings Bond program has promoted savings, we used aggregated data provided by IRS on income tax filers who used at least part of their tax refunds to buy paper savings bonds from 2010 through 2013. We used the data to determine the number of tax filers who bought paper savings bonds, including those with adjusted gross incomes of $25,000 or below, and the amount of savings bonds they purchased. We also reviewed IRS documentation, including IRS Form 8888, Allocation of Refund (Including Savings Bond Purchases. We interviewed Treasury and IRS officials about the Tax Time program's operations, benefits, and costs. In addition, we interviewed nonprofit organizations that had promoted savings bonds as a savings vehicle or collaborated with Treasury on efforts to improve access to financial products and services about the benefits of the program.

To examine the extent to which lower-income households are saving using financial products, we used data from the Survey of Consumer Finances (SCF) issued by the Board of Governors of the Federal Reserve System for survey years 2001, 2004, 2007, 2010, and 2013 to estimate, among other things, the percentage of U.S. households holding financial assets, including U.S. savings bonds, and the median value of such financial assets held by U.S. households.[1] We chose these survey years because they covered more than 10 years before the discontinuation of the sale of paper savings bonds at financial institutions but also one year after the change. To identify and describe the government and nonprofit programs developed to promote savings by lower-income households, we conducted research on and reviewed select federal, state, local, and nonprofit programs targeting either long-term (such as retirement or asset accumulation) or short-term savings goals for lower-income households. We also interviewed officials from six federal agencies involved in the Financial Literacy and Education Commission, state and local government agencies, and nonprofit organizations and academics focusing on savings and asset-building programs.[2]

We assessed the reliability of the data we used in each of the three objectives by reviewing documentation, such as Treasury's description of the data in the monthly statement of public debt, SCF codebooks, and Federal Reserve bulletins on the SCF. We also interviewed knowledgeable officials, and conducted testing on relevant data fields where applicable, such as the number of tax filers participating in the Tax Time program and amounts of savings bonds purchased. We found the data we reviewed to be sufficiently reliable for the purposes of our analyses.

We conducted this performance audit from August 2014 to July 2015 in accordance with generally accepted government auditing standards. Those standards require that we plan and perform the audit to obtain sufficient, appropriate evidence to provide a reasonable basis for our findings and conclusions based on our audit objectives. We believe that the evidence obtained provides a reasonable basis for our findings and conclusions based on our audit objectives.

BACKGROUND

Treasury has issued savings bonds since 1935. Savings bonds offer investors the ability to purchase securities with lower minimum denominations than those for marketable Treasury securities.[3] When individuals purchase savings bonds, they loan the amount they paid for the bonds to the U.S. government. Over a period of time (up to 30 years), the savings bonds earn interest and, after 12 months of their original purchase, can be cashed in for their purchase price, plus the interest they have earned, subject to a 3-month interest penalty during the first 5 years. Over the years, Treasury has offered a number of savings bonds with different terms and interest rates. Currently, Treasury offers Series EE bonds, which have a fixed interest rate, and Series I bonds, which pay an interest rate that is tied to inflation.[4] Savings bonds do not represent a major source of funds for the Treasury.

The Bureau of the Fiscal Service, one of Treasury's 10 bureaus, helps to fund the federal government by selling Treasury securities, including savings bonds. Treasury Securities Services within the bureau operates Treasury's Retail Securities program, which allows retail investors to purchase savings bonds and marketable securities in electronic form directly from Treasury. The office's flagship system is TreasuryDirect, an online proprietary system created in 2002 that allows customers to buy and hold savings bonds and marketable securities, and to manage their accounts without assistance from a customer service representative. TreasuryDirect customers can purchase securities at any time, direct electronic payments to bank accounts, and convert paper savings bonds to electronic savings bonds in the same series and with the same issue date. TreasuryDirect customers also can set up payroll deductions and automatically recurring purchases. As of March 2015, TreasuryDirect had around 580,700 accounts that were funded and held nearly $27 billion.[5]

TREASURY ELIMINATED PAPER SAVINGS BONDS TO REDUCE COSTS BUT CREATED CHALLENGES FOR SOME SAVINGS BOND INVESTORS

The elimination of paper savings bonds reduced program costs but made purchasing bonds more difficult for some savers. However, our analysis of Treasury's bond data showed that the drop in bond purchases after the elimination of paper savings bonds was not statistically significant. As shown in Figure 1, annual purchases of U.S. savings bonds declined significantly from 2001 through 2013, falling from around $14.6 billion to less than $1 billion, or by more than 90 percent.[6] Over this period, savings bond purchases declined every year, except from 2002 to 2003. Likewise, the role of savings bonds in helping to fund the federal debt also declined over the period, accounting for about 3.2 percent of the federal debt in 2001 and about 1.0 percent in 2013.

Consistent with the decline in savings bond purchases, the percentage of U.S. households holding savings bonds and the amount of savings bonds these households hold also have declined. On the basis of data from the Federal Reserve Board's SCF, we found that around 17 percent of households held savings bonds in 2001, with a median value of $1,300 for those who held them (fig. 2). In 2013, around 10 percent of households held savings bonds with a median value of $1,000 for those who held them.[7]

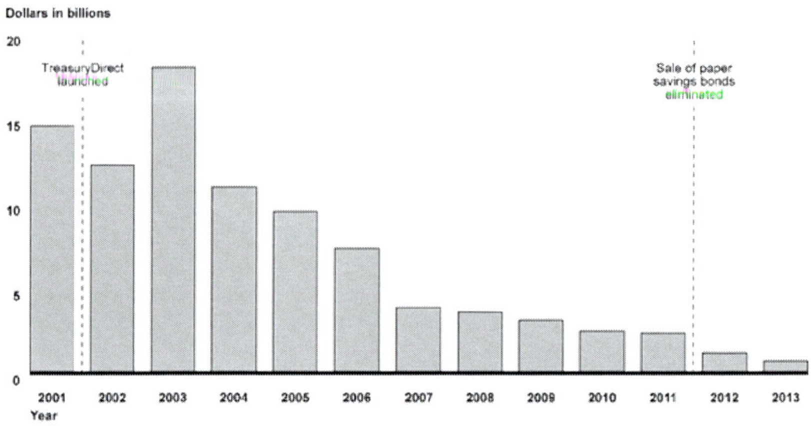

Source: GAO analysis of Treasury savings bond data. | GAO-15-563.

Note: We adjusted the monthly savings bonds purchased for inflation using the consumer price index, with June 2014 as the base month, before aggregating purchases by year.

Figure 1. Purchases of U.S. Savings Bonds from 2001 through 2013. (in 2014 Dollars)

Moreover, savings bonds as a percentage of total financial assets held by U.S. households declined from 0.7 percent to 0.3 percent over the same period.

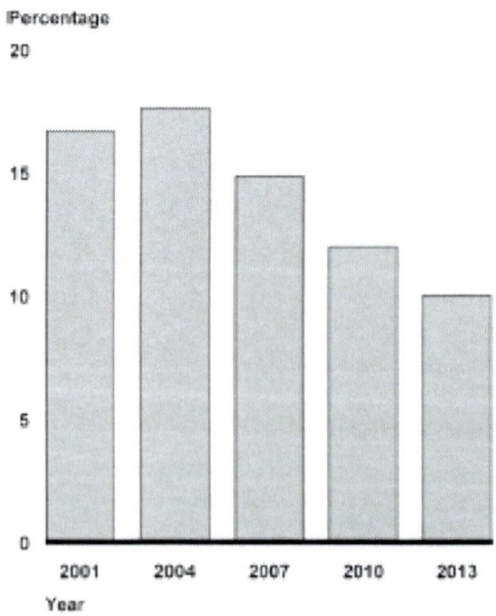

Source: GAO analysis of 2001 through 2013 Survey of Consumer Finances data. | GAO-15-563.

Figure 2. Percentage of U.S. Households Holding Savings Bonds from 2001 through 2013.

Treasury Eliminated Paper Savings Bonds to Reduce Program Costs and Provide Other Benefits

Following the long-term decline in savings bond purchases, Treasury stopped selling paper savings bonds through over-the-counter channels, including through financial institutions and mail-in orders, on January 1, 2012, as part of its agency-wide electronic initiative to reduce program costs and improve customer service. According to Treasury officials, the agency phased out the issuance of paper savings bonds through employer-sponsored payroll savings plans in 2010, and the ending of savings bond sales through over-the-counter channels was the last step of discontinuing paper savings bonds. Treasury estimated that the elimination of over-the-counter sales of paper savings bonds would save nearly $70 million in program costs from 2012 through 2016. Treasury calculated these savings by estimating how much it would save in costs associated with issuing new paper bonds and servicing and redeeming existing paper bonds, which include fees paid to banks, postage, and printing. For example, Treasury estimated that the change would eliminate around $14.5 million in fees paid to financial institutions for issuing and redeeming savings bonds and around $12.7 million in postage expenses for mailing paper bonds to customers over the 5-year period. Additionally, Treasury estimated that it would save in personnel costs because fewer employees would be needed to process customer service transactions. According to Treasury's estimates, the change would save around $4.9 million in compensation and benefit costs for Treasury staff and $28.5 million in Federal Reserve Bank personnel costs over the 5-year period. Finally, Treasury estimated $9 million in savings from reductions in paper stock, overhead, forms, and other costs.

In addition to the cost savings, Treasury expected the change to provide customer benefits, such as increased security and convenience. Although paper bonds allowed buyers to purchase savings bonds at financial institutions, Treasury's online system for purchasing savings bonds and other Treasury securities—TreasuryDirect—allows customers to buy, manage, and redeem savings bonds electronically at any time. Treasury officials told us that electronic bonds are safer and more secure, because paper bonds could be lost, stolen, altered, or fraudulently redeemed. Treasury officials also added that electronic bonds provide the agency with both operational advantages and enhanced customer experience, since Treasury can automatically track bond purchases, redemptions, and values for the customer.

Eliminating Paper Savings Bonds Has Created Challenges for Some Bond Buyers

When Treasury eliminated paper savings bonds, it created access challenges for bond buyers who do not have a bank account and Internet access. Customers now must use TreasuryDirect to purchase electronic savings bonds, although some can purchase paper savings bonds through the Tax Time program, which we discuss later in this report. To open a TreasuryDirect account, a customer generally must have both Internet access and a bank account. While TreasuryDirect can be accessed through cellular phones and other mobile devices, the website is not optimized for such use. According to representatives from a nonprofit organization that focuses on savings for lower-income households, mobile access is the primary means of Internet access for some lower-income consumers. According to 2011 Census Bureau data, around 50 percent of households with less than $25,000 in income did not have computer-based Internet access from some location.[8] Further, according to the 2013 Federal Deposit Insurance Corporation's (FDIC) National Survey of Unbanked and Underbanked Households, 7.7 percent of U.S. households, or nearly 9.6 million households, were unbanked—that is, they did not have a bank account at an insured institution.[9] As a result, such households or individuals may not be able to access TreasuryDirect or complete a transaction if they wanted to buy savings bonds.

Treasury officials recognized the access challenges related to TreasuryDirect that some potential users might face, but told us such challenges could be mitigated. Treasury officials said that they worked with organizations that provided Internet access to the public, such as libraries and community centers, and determined that such organizations provide the level of Internet access required for potential TreasuryDirect users. The officials also told us that in lieu of a bank account, individuals could use reloadable debit cards to purchase and redeem savings bonds through TreasuryDirect. While the use of such cards provides an avenue for those without a traditional bank account to purchase savings bonds, Treasury estimated that few savings bonds, approximately 1,426, had been purchased using prepaid debit cards from mid-April 2005 through mid-November 2014. Further, Treasury officials told us that unbanked individuals could use the Tax Time program to purchase paper savings bonds. Our analysis of IRS data on the Tax Time program indicates that around 91 percent of tax filers who used part of their tax refund to purchase paper savings bonds had part of their refund directly deposited into a bank account. Similarly, based on data from SCF surveys from 2001 through

2010, over 90 percent of households who owned savings bonds have bank accounts. Additionally, according to FDIC's survey, more than 90 percent of all households the agency surveyed had a bank account.

According to Treasury officials and representatives from several nonprofit organizations that we interviewed, TreasuryDirect also poses some usability challenges. For example, Treasury officials and nonprofit representatives told us that giving savings bonds as a gift through TreasuryDirect can be a cumbersome process. They explained that TreasuryDirect requires the individual buying the savings bond to have the Social Security number and TreasuryDirect account number of the recipient of the gift bond, information the individual may not know. The gifting process also requires the recipients or their parents or guardians to set up a TreasuryDirect account, if they do not have one. Treasury officials told us that issues associated with the process of buying bonds as gifts were the source of the most common complaints from customers about savings bond transactions through TreasuryDirect. In addition, representatives from nonprofit organizations and an academic we interviewed told us that TreasuryDirect generally was not a user-friendly system, even for individuals who were comfortable using the Internet for their financial transactions. They told us that navigating the system was not easy and could pose challenges to potential customers who were not familiar with online financial transactions. Similarly, Treasury officials told us that customers anecdotally had expressed concerns about difficult navigation, lengthy application pages, organization of information, security features, complicated linked accounts processes, and difficulty locating tax reporting information. When Treasury eliminated paper savings bonds in January 2012, there were nearly 379,000 total funded TreasuryDirect accounts.[10] As of the end of March 2015, there were over 580,000 total funded TreasuryDirect accounts, but the extent to which the increase resulted from savings bond investors has not been determined.

Decline in Purchases after the Elimination of Paper Savings Bonds Is Consistent with Long-Term Trends, and Treasury Is Addressing Access and Usability Challenges

Our analyses of Treasury savings bond data indicated that the decline in savings bond purchases after Treasury discontinued the sale of paper savings bonds in January 2012 was consistent with the overall long-term decline in savings bond purchases. In addition, the decline since January 2012 generally was not statistically significant based on models we estimated. While there was a large decline in purchases in 2012 and 2013 when sales of paper savings bonds were discontinued, there are a number of factors that could account for this decline. For example, savings bond purchases declined in 9 out of 10 years from 2002 to 2011, and some declines were quite large, hence recent declines in purchases may be reflective of long-term trends. In addition, we found that savings bond purchases have been sensitive to interest rate changes, with savers typically purchasing more when interest rates are higher and purchasing less when they are lower. The low interest rates in recent years may account for some of the decline in savings bond purchases.

Although lower-income households that do not have bank accounts or Internet access could face challenges accessing or using TreasuryDirect, this challenge may only affect a small percentage of such households. Our analyses indicate that a small percentage of such households buy savings bonds in general, even when they were available in paper form. According to data from the 2013 SCF survey, 4.6 percent of lower-income households held savings bonds in 2013, and this percentage had declined from 7.7 percent in 2001.

In a July 2014 Federal Register release, and in support of its strategy to reach new customers, develop new product delivery streams, and increase the number of available product offerings, Treasury released its plans to introduce the Treasury Retail Investment Manager (TRIM), which will replace TreasuryDirect.[11] According to Treasury officials, TRIM will be more flexible and responsive to changing business and digital investing needs. Treasury officials told us that they plan to offer mobile phone access through TRIM, which could improve access for households that do not have computer-based Internet access at home. Treasury officials also told us that TRIM would attempt to address a number of TreasuryDirect's usability challenges. For example, Treasury officials told us that the TRIM system should be more user friendly for customers, because it will have an online interface that is similar to the online interfaces that banks and stock brokers offer and with which most customers are likely familiar. The system also is expected to streamline various steps for customers navigating the system—for example when they open or sign into accounts—to improve usability and potentially save Treasury money by reducing calls to customer service.

According to Treasury officials, they also are exploring ways for TRIM to simplify the process for buying savings bonds as gifts and to allow for multiple funding options. One option under consideration is for a customer to buy a savings bond gift certificate that can be given to another individual, who can go online to open a TRIM account and use the certificate to buy the savings bond directly. Treasury also is exploring multiple funding options for customer accounts to provide options to savers who do not have bank accounts.

As of May 2015, TRIM was under development, and Treasury officials told us that its release date had not been set. According to Treasury officials, TRIM is being developed in four phases—initiation, planning, execution, and closing. Treasury officials told us that TRIM was in the planning phase and that the system's design was being developed. Specifically, Treasury officials are working on defining technical requirements for the system. Before TRIM can be implemented, Treasury will need to complete the execution and closing phases, which include technical design, system coding, various testing, consumer education, and system documentation. Treasury officials told us that they did not have a specific release date for TRIM, which will depend on the time needed to complete the next steps in the project plan. According to a Treasury estimate issued in 2013, TRIM was expected to cost around $18 million to develop and implement. Treasury officials told us that, as of May 2015, they did not have any changes to this estimate and that the costs they had incurred thus far had been consistent with the estimate. They also told us that Treasury had tentative plans to develop an implementation plan for TRIM by April 2016.

TAX TIME PROGRAM PROMOTES SAVINGS, BUT TREASURY HAS NOT CONSIDERED COSTS ALONG WITH BENEFITS IN ITS ANNUAL DECISIONS TO EXTEND THE PROGRAM

Since 2010, U.S. tax filers have used the Tax Time program to save by using their tax refund to purchase paper savings bonds. For example, about 55,000 tax filers with adjusted gross incomes of $25,000 or less participated in the program for tax years 2010 through 2013 and bought about $13.7 million in savings bonds. Treasury has been extending the program annually in consideration of some of the program's benefits, but not in consideration of the program's costs.

Tax Time Savings Bond Program Promotes Savings through the Purchase of Paper Savings Bonds, Including by Lower-Income Households

Since 2010, U.S. tax filers have been able to use their tax refund to purchase paper savings bonds through the Tax Time Savings Bond program. In 2009, President Obama proposed a package of initiatives to spur increased savings that included a provision for purchasing savings bonds with tax returns. Under the Tax Time program, tax filers receiving a tax refund may use an IRS form to allocate their refund among several options, such as purchasing paper savings bonds or depositing their refund directly into their bank account.[12] As shown in Table 1, in tax years 2010 through 2013 about 142,000 total tax filers used the Tax Time program to buy a total of about $72.5 million in paper savings bonds.[13] (According to data provided by Treasury, of the 142,000 total tax filers that used the Tax Time program, about 20 percent were repeat participants in the program). These filers purchased, on average, approximately $500 in paper savings bonds each year. Table 1 also shows that about 55,000 tax filers with an adjusted gross income of $25,000 or less collectively bought about $13.7 million in paper savings bonds. These filers purchased, on average, approximately $250 in paper savings bonds each year. At the same time, the number of tax filers participating in the Tax Time program and the amount of savings bonds purchased under the program were relatively small. The total number of tax filers receiving a refund for tax years 2010 through 2013 was more than 100 million in each year, and Tax Time participants made up less than 1 percent of this group. Similarly, the amount of savings bonds purchased through the program from 2010 through 2013 accounted for about 1 percent of the total amount of all savings bonds purchased during those years.

About 30 percent of Tax Time program participants also were tax filers who received the Earned Income Tax Credit. Enacted by Congress in 1975, the Earned Income Tax Credit is one of the largest antipoverty programs.[14] Generally, income and family size determine a taxpayer's eligibility, and the credit is a refundable tax credit for low-to-moderate income working individuals and couples—particularly those with children. As shown in Table 2, about 30 percent of tax filers participating in the program from 2010 through 2013 received the Earned Income Tax Credit.

Table 1. Number of Tax Filers Purchasing Savings Bonds through the Tax Time Savings Bond Program and Amounts Purchased, Tax Years 2010-2013[a]

Tax year	Total number of tax filers purchasing paper savings bonds[b]	Total amount of paper savings bonds purchased	Number of tax filers with an adjusted gross income of $25,000 or less purchasing paper savings bonds[b]	Amount of paper savings bonds purchased by tax filers with an adjusted gross income of $25,000or less
2010c	32,449	$11,524,200	13,724	$3,151,371
2011	39,417	21,565,850	15,280	3,715,089
2012	36,263	21,537,450	13,369	3,493,656
2013d	33,990	17,845,500	12,655	3,297,552
Total	142,119	$72,473,000	55,028	$13,657,668

Source: GAO analysis of IRS data. l GAO-15-563.

[a]Since Tax Time program data for tax year 2014 would not be available until after the 2015 tax filing season, the latest tax year for which we obtained Tax Time program data was 2013.

[b]We calculated the number of tax filers for these categories by aggregating IRS data on the total number of tax returns filed for tax years 2010 through 2013. Since some tax filers participated in the program in more than one year, the number of unique tax filers is less than the total provided in this table.

[c]For tax year 2010, IRS had data only on the amount of paper savings bonds tax filers asked to purchase and not the actual purchase figures. IRS officials explained that in almost all cases, the requests went through and were processed for the exact amount requested.

[d]For tax year 2013, IRS provided us with totals on tax returns filed through April 24, 2014. Data on tax returns with an adjusted gross income of $25,000 or less are based on tax returns filed through October 23, 2014.

According to representatives from three nonprofit organizations and two academics we interviewed, tax season provides an opportunity for tax filers receiving a refund to set aside an amount of money specifically for savings. They told us that tax season was often the one time during the year that tax filers—particularly those with low incomes—had a relatively large lump sum of money available to save. However, in some instances, tax filers receiving a refund may already know what they plan to use their refunds for, and that may not include any savings.

Table 2. Number and Percentage of Tax Filers Purchasing Paper Savings Bonds through the Tax Time Program and Receiving the Earned Income Tax Credit, Tax Years 2010-2013[a]

Tax year	Total number of tax filers purchasing paper savings bonds[b]	Total number of tax filers purchasing paper savings bonds and receiving Earned Income Tax Credit[b]	Percentage of tax filers purchasing paper savings bonds receiving Earned Income Tax Credit (%)
2010	32,449	10,347	32
2011	39,417	11,463	29
2012	36,263	10,405	29
2013[c]	33,990	10,092	30
Total	142,119	42,307	30

Source: GAO analysis of IRS data. l GAO-15-563.

[a]Since Tax Time program data for tax year 2014 would not be available until after the 2015 tax filing season, the latest tax year for which we obtained Tax Time program data was 2013.

[b]We calculated the number of tax filers for these categories by aggregating IRS data on the total number of tax returns filed for tax years 2010 through 2013. Since some tax filers participated in the program in more than one year, the number of unique tax filers is less than the total provided in this table.

[c]For tax year 2013, IRS provided us with totals on tax returns filed through April 24, 2014. Data on total tax returns that were filed after April 24, 2014, and included requests to purchase paper savings bonds are not included in the totals in this table.

Treasury Plans to Extend the Tax Time Program in the Short-Term, but Has Not Considered Program Costs Along with the Benefits

Treasury has been extending the Tax Time program on an annual basis and plans to continue extending it in the short term. According to Treasury officials, the program was scheduled to expire after the 2015 tax season, in which case tax filers would no longer have had the option to use the IRS form to purchase paper savings bonds.[15] However, Treasury officials told us that the agency decided in December 2014 to extend the program through the 2016 tax season. The decision was made by the Fiscal Assistant Secretary of the Treasury based on an internal recommendation from the Commissioner of the

Bureau of the Fiscal Service, which oversees the savings bond program. Treasury officials said that they intended to continue recommending the continuation of paper tax-time bonds until a suitable electronic alternative is implemented. However, Treasury officials did not provide us with any additional information on how an electronic alternative would replace the option of purchasing paper savings bonds. For participants who do not have Internet access or want to buy bonds electronically, it is not clear what a suitable electronic alternative would be.

Although Treasury has been extending the Tax Time program on an annual basis, it has not assessed the program's costs along with its benefits. In deciding to extend the program in the last 2 years, Treasury officials told us that they considered participation levels and the amount of savings bonds purchased through the program. Such data indicate some of the program's benefits, namely its ability to promote savings by lower-income and other households. While the amount of bonds purchased and program participation levels can be quantified, other benefits of the program, such as providing a savings opportunity for lower-income households that may not be able to access TreasuryDirect to purchase savings bonds online, are more difficult to quantify. Although Treasury officials considered some of the Tax Time program's benefits in deciding to extend it, they generally did not consider the program's costs in their decision-making process. According to Treasury and IRS officials, Treasury has not conducted an analysis on the current costs of the program or determined how much Treasury would save if the program were allowed to expire after the 2016 tax season. IRS officials told us that IRS's current costs to administer the program were minimal, because IRS largely processes the forms electronically. Treasury officials told us that its current cost of printing and mailing a paper savings bond was approximately 17 cents, but this estimate did not include the share of the overhead, system, and other costs attributable to paper savings bonds. Moreover, the 17 cent estimate also did not include any cost that IRS incurred for its role in implementing the program.

In prior work on agency stewardship of public funds, we reported that properly estimating program costs is necessary for several reasons and that comparing these costs to the program's benefits to evaluate alternatives related to program decisions is a best practice.[16] Producing cost estimates is important for evaluating resources and making decisions about programs at key decision points. Credible cost estimates also help support funding decisions for an agency's programs. Comparing these costs to the benefits in order to consider all alternatives for a program ensures linkage between the alternatives.

In deciding to extend the Tax Time program, Treasury has considered some of the program's benefits but generally not the program's costs, both of which are needed to evaluate program performance and alternatives. As discussed, Treasury has previously considered levels of program participation and amounts of savings bonds purchased by participants in its decisions, and most recently has extended the program until a suitable electronic alternative is available. Consideration of not only the Tax Time program's benefits but also the program's cost would provide Treasury with important information in evaluating not only the resource requirements when deciding whether to allow the program to expire but also the program's performance in relation to its benefits and costs. For example, if the program's operating costs are minimal, then the program's benefits may outweigh its costs, such as providing opportunities for lower-income households to save. Conversely, if program costs are significant, those costs might outweigh the program's benefits in light of the number of tax filers using the program and the availability of an electronic alternative. However, by not having full, reliable, estimates of the cost of the Tax Time program to compare to the benefits, Treasury's ability to make a fully informed decision is limited.

Savings by Lower-Income Households Are Limited but Federal Agencies and Other Entities Have Created Savings Programs

GAO found that lower-income households save relatively small amounts and face a number of savings challenges that result, in part, from limited access to financial institutions and products. According to several academics and nonprofits we interviewed, savings and other asset-building programs are fundamental building blocks for helping lower income-households achieve economic mobility and security. Savings provide a buffer against unexpected events and a means to move up the economic ladder through investments, such as by buying a home, paying for college, starting a business, or saving for retirement. In addition to the Tax Time program, discussed above, federal, state, and local agencies as well as nonprofits have developed a number of programs aimed at assisting lower-income households to save and build assets. These programs include providing financial literacy and education services, and range from promoting short-term financial goals, such as emergency savings, to long-term financial goals, such as saving for retirement.[17]

Lower-income Households Have Limited Financial Assets and May Have Difficulty Saving

According to 2013 SCF data, lower-income households have limited savings in bank accounts and other financial assets.[18] U.S. households in the lowest income quintile (or bottom fifth) had a median income of around $14,200 in 2013, and households in the next income quintile had a median income of around $28,400.[19] As shown in Table 3, 82 percent and 93 percent of the U.S. households in the bottom two income quintiles had financial assets, but the median value of these financial assets were $550 and $3,064, respectively. In other words, half of the households in the lowest income quintile held $550 or less in financial assets. In comparison, the median value for financial assets for all surveyed households in 2013 was $17,580. Bank accounts are the mostly widely held financial asset among lower-income households, according to 2013 SCF data. However, separate from bank accounts, a significant majority of lower-income households hold few or no other financial assets, such as stocks, bonds, or mutual funds. For example, 9 percent of U.S. households in the bottom income quintile have retirement accounts, compared with around 28 percent of households in the next lowest income quintile.

As shown in Figure 3, median household financial assets, excluding retirement accounts, dropped in the wake of the 2001 and 2008 recessions and have not recovered to pre-recession levels. Median holdings in 2013 were down by 40 percent or more in comparison to median holdings in 2001 for both the population as a whole and for lower-income households.[20] The median value of non-retirement financial assets for the two lowest income quintiles was $1,000 in 2013. This total reflects the relatively low level of short-term savings for these households.

Some lower-income households faced challenges obtaining financial or banking services although SCF data indicate that most lower-income households have a bank account. For example, the 2013 FDIC Survey reported that a majority of unbanked households reported not having enough money to maintain an account or meet a minimum balance. Such households may use alternative financial services providers, such as nonbank check cashers, payday lenders, or pawn shops.

Table 3. 2013 Survey of Consumer Finances Holdings of Financial Assets by Household Income

Household percentile of the US income distribution	Percent of households with any financial assets	Total household financial assets		Percent of households with any checking, savings, or other transaction account
		Median[a]	Mean [b]	
Less than 20	82%	$550	$25,951	79%
20-39.9	93%	$3,064	$39,751	91%
All households	95%	$17,580	$253,190	93%

Source: 2013 SCF data. l GAO-15-563.

Note: Based on 2013 SCF data, we defined lower-income households as the lower two distributions (or quintiles) of households in the United States.

[a]The 95 percent confidence interval on the median holdings of financial assets were $15,744 to $19,416 for the population as a whole, $454 to $646 for the households with income below the 20th percentile, and $2,310 to $3,818 for households with income between the 20th and 39th percentiles.

[b]The 95 percent confidence interval on the mean financial assets in the population as a whole is $240,459 to $265,920. For households with income below the 20th percentile of the U.S. income distribution, the 95 percent confidence interval around the mean financial assets is $14,205 to $37,697. For households with income in at least the 20th percentiles and below the 40th percentile, the 95 percent confidence interval around the mean financial assets is $32,402 to $47,100.

According to the 2013 FDIC Survey and the 2013 SCF, less than 10 percent of households are unbanked. In addition, one in five households (or 20 percent) were underbanked in 2013—underbanked households are those that have a bank account but have also used alternative financial services from non-bank providers in the last 12 months.[21] The highest unbanked rates continued to be found among non-Asian minorities, lower-income households, younger households, and unemployed households.

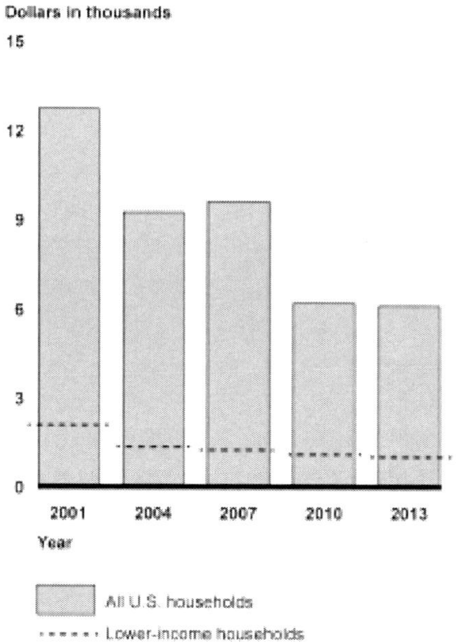

Source: GAO analysis of 2001 through 2013 Survey if Consumer Finances data. | GAO-15-563.

Note: The 95 percent confidence interval on the median holdings of non-retirement financial assets for the population as a whole were: $11,288 to $14,130 in 2001, $7,736 to $10,589 in 2004, $8,651 to $10,432 in 2007, $5,651 to $6,742 in 2010, and $5,631 to $6,569 in 2013. The 95 percent confidence interval on the median holdings of non-retirement financial assets for the bottom two income quintiles were: $1,636 to $2,461 in 2001, $1,090 to $1,658 in 2004, $1,079 to $1,607 in 2007, $988 to $1,156 in 2010, and $936 to $1,064 in 2013.

Figure 3. 2001 to 2013 Survey of Consumer Finances Median Holdings of Financial Assets, Excluding Retirement Accounts.

Federal Agencies Generally Focus on Promoting Financial Literacy, but Some Are Involved in Savings Programs

Since at least 2003, the federal government has played a broad role in promoting financial literacy, which encompasses financial education—the process by which individuals improve their knowledge and understanding of financial products, services, and concepts. Financial literacy plays an important role in helping to promote the financial health and stability of individuals and families. In prior work on financial literacy, we reported that federal agencies have made progress in recent years in coordinating their financial literacy activities and collaborating with nonfederal entities, in large part due to the efforts of the federal multiagency Financial Literacy and Education Commission (FLEC).[22]

In addition to their financial literacy efforts, some federal agencies have developed savings programs involving financial assets. These programs are aimed at helping households and individuals that may not have access to traditional savings vehicles, such as employer-sponsored retirement plans.

myRA®

According to a Treasury official, Treasury launched the *my*RA program, which is in a soft-launch phase, to promote retirement savings among individuals without access to employer-sponsored retirement plans.[23] According to Treasury, the program offers a retirement savings account that is a Roth IRA, so it follows the same rules that apply generally to Roth IRAs and receives the same tax treatment.[24] A *my*RA has no fees, no minimum-amount requirement, a maximum balance of $15,000, and it can be funded through payroll direct deposit. The account houses a savings bond that will never go down in value (except from withdrawals) and the security in the account, like other Treasury securities, is backed by the U.S. Treasury. Participating employers make *my*RA information available to their employees. Employees are able to enroll in the program, and then elect to have a portion of each paycheck directly deposited into their *my*RA automatically.

Treasury officials stated that they worked to develop the framework for this program in 2014, including issuing a new Treasury security to serve as the investment option for these accounts, and designing easy-to understand materials for savers. Treasury continued to build on the development process by making *my*RA available to a small group of employers, including federal agencies. Presently, Treasury is working closely with this small group of participants to get feedback and better ensure that the user experience is as simple and straightforward as possible–both for employers and employees–before *my*RA becomes more broadly available later this year. Treasury has indicated that it is too early to begin evaluating the impact of the *my*RA program. However, Treasury officials told us that they will continue to monitor the progress of the program as it moves through its soft-launch phase.

Money Smart and Model Safe Account Programs

Given the challenges low-and-moderate income households face in obtaining financial or banking services, FDIC has created a number of initiatives to help low and moderate-income individuals improve their financial skills and use financial institutions according to FDIC officials. For example, FDIC officials stated that, in 2001, FDIC developed the Money Smart program, which is a comprehensive financial education curriculum designed to help consumers, especially low- and- moderate income consumers and entrepreneurs, enhance their financial skills and help create positive banking relationships. Officials added that FDIC provides the curriculum free of charge in formats for consumers to complete on their own or through instructor-led classes.[25] According to FDIC, the program has reached over 2.75 million consumers since 2001. In April 2007, FDIC used a three-part survey to determine the effectiveness of its Money Smart financial education curriculum and found that the program positively influenced how course participants managed their finances and their financial confidence.[26] The study also found that these positive changes were sustained months after participants had completed Money Smart training. Specifically, the study found that participants were more likely to open deposit accounts, save money in a mainstream deposit product, use and adhere to a budget, and demonstrate increased confidence in their financial abilities when they were contacted 6 to 12 months after completing the Money Smart course compared to before beginning the course.

To further promote low and moderate income consumers' access to financial services, FDIC developed the Model Safe Accounts Pilot in January 2011. The pilot was designed to evaluate the feasibility of having financial institutions offer safe, low-cost transaction and savings accounts (Safe Accounts) that are responsive to the needs of underserved consumers- including those with low and moderate incomes. Nine financial institutions participated in the pilot by offering Safe Accounts, which are checkless, card-based electronic accounts that limit acquisition and maintenance costs. These accounts allow withdrawals only through automated teller machines, point-of-sale terminals, automated clearinghouse pre-authorizations, and other automated means. Overdraft and nonsufficient funds fees are prohibited with the transaction accounts. According to FDIC, the nine banks opened more than 3,500 Safe Accounts during the pilot. Retention of these accounts exceeded expectations—more than 80 percent of transaction accounts and 95 percent of savings accounts remained open at the end of the 1-year pilot period.[27] According to FDIC, Safe Accounts performed on par with or better than other transaction and savings accounts and several of the banks plan to continue to offer Safe Accounts—some banks are also considering the possibility of graduating pilot accountholders to traditional deposit accounts. Although the Safe Accounts program was only a 1-year pilot, FDIC officials told us that the agency provides interested FDIC insured institutions with a Safe Accounts template that includes guidelines for offering cost-effective transactional and savings accounts to underserved consumers. This template was based, in part, on lessons learned during the pilot phase.

Youth Savings Pilot Program

FDIC announced its Youth Savings Pilot Program on August 4, 2014. According to FDIC, this pilot program seeks to identify and highlight promising approaches to offering financial education tied to the opening of safe, low-cost savings accounts for school-aged children. The pilot has two phases. According to FDIC officials, Phase I includes FDIC insured institutions currently working with schools or nonprofit organizations that help students open savings accounts in conjunction with financial education programs during the 2014 to 2015 and 2015 to 2016 school years. Nine banks differing in size, location, and business models were selected for the first phase. The officials added that Phase II will include FDIC insured institutions beginning or expanding youth savings account programs during the 2015 to 2016 school year. FDIC is collecting summary information—including data on the number of accounts opened and financial education approaches used—from pilot participants. When the pilot is complete, FDIC intends to publish a report to provide financial institutions with promising approaches to working with schools and other organizations to combine financial education with access to a savings account.

Assets for Independence Program

The Office of Community Services at the Department of Health and Human Services' Administration for Children and Families administers the Assets for Independence program. Started in 1998, the Assets for Independence program awards grants to community-based entities, nonprofits and state, local, and tribal government agencies that partner with nonprofits to implement an asset-based approach for assisting low income families to become economically self-sufficient according to the Administration for Children and Families.[28] According to agency officials, entities receiving these grants enroll participants in Assets for Independence projects to save earned income in special-purpose, matched savings accounts, also called individual development accounts. According to agency officials, every dollar that a participant deposits into an Assets for Independence individual development account is matched by the Assets for Independence project. Match rates can vary from $1 in match funds for every $1 the participant deposits in his or her individual development account, to as much as $8 in match funds for every $1 saved. Participants generally must use their individual development accounts and matching funds for a qualified expense: the purchase of a home; the capitalization or expansion of a business; or post-secondary educational expenses.[29] According to agency officials, under the program, grantees are required to assist participants in the demonstration project in obtaining the skills necessary to achieve economic self-sufficiency. Examples of such activities include providing financial education and credit counseling.

As illustrated in Table 4, from 2010 through 2014, according to agency officials the Administration for Children and Families awarded 269 Assets for Independence grants and over $62 million to a number of organizations including nonprofits, state or local governments, tribal governments, and community development financial institutions, to name a few. Table 4 also shows that the program budget for the Administration for Children and Families since fiscal year 2010.

Table 4. Assets for Independence Grant Awards and Budget Authority for Fiscal Years 2010-2014

Year	Number of grants awarded	Total amount awarded (Dollars in thousands)	Budget authority (Dollars in thousands)
2010	53	$11,240	$23,907
2011	66	$15,480	$23,977
2012	61	$13,595	$19,869
2013	45	$12,699	$18,593
2014	44	$9,974	$18,950
Total	269	$62,988	$105,296

Source: Administration for Children and Families. | GAO-15-563.

According to Administration for Children and Families data through fiscal year 2010, more than 90 percent of Assets for Independence projects allowed participants to pursue homeownership as an asset goal, while more than 80 percent allowed participants to pursue postsecondary education or training and business capitalization as asset goals. Nearly one-third of projects allowed participants to transfer account savings to the individual development account of a spouse or dependent.

In 2011, Administration for Children and Families began a random assignment evaluation of the Assets for Independence program at two grantee sites. This evaluation will assess the impact of Assets for Independence program participation on savings, savings patterns, and asset purchase by lower-income individuals and families. It builds on the previous quasi-experimental evaluation and studies of other non-Assets for Independence funded individual development account projects. The 2008 evaluation used data from the early to mid-2000s and found that Assets for Independence program participants were 35 percent more likely to become homeowners, 84 percent more likely to become business owners, and nearly twice as likely to pursue post-secondary education or training compared with a corresponding national sample of nonparticipants eligible for the program. According to the Administration for Children and Families, the random assignment evaluation will further understanding of the program's overall impact on early participant outcomes. The evaluation team completed participant enrollment and baseline data collection in July 2014 and expects to release its final report in early 2016.

Family Self Sufficiency Program

The Department of Housing and Urban Development (HUD) awards competitive grants to public housing agencies for the administration of programs that encourage residents of public housing to attain self-sufficiency through programs such as the Family Self Sufficiency program.[30] The program funds coordinators who help participants achieve employment goals and accumulate assets. Through the coordination and linkage to local service providers, program participants receive training and counseling that enables them to increase their earned income and decrease or reduce their need for rental assistance. Under the Family Self Sufficiency program, escrow accounts are used as incentives to increase work effort and earnings. Specifically, when participants have to pay a higher rent after their earned income increases, the public housing agency calculates an escrow credit that is deposited each month into an interest-bearing account (see fig. 4). Families that successfully complete their contract for the Family Self Sufficiency program receive their accrued escrow funds.

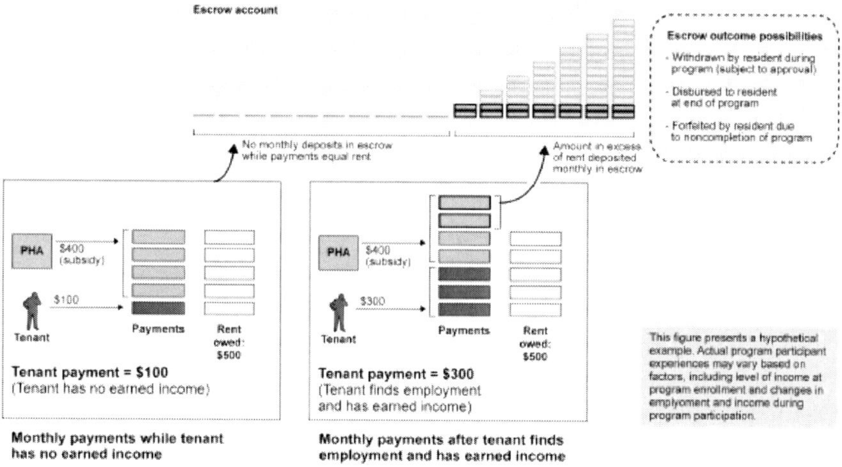

Soure: GAO. GAO-15-563.

Figure 4. HUD Family Self Sufficiency Program Escrow Account Example.

According to HUD officials, over 72,000 households participated in the program in fiscal year 2014, and 4,382 families successfully completed their Family Self Sufficiency contracts. The 2013, 2014 and 2015 appropriation amounts for the Family Self Sufficiency program was $75 million.[31] HUD is requesting $85 million in 2016.

In September 2004, HUD commissioned a 5-year prospective study of the Family Self Sufficiency program, focusing on programs serving Housing Choice Voucher recipients. [32]

The study provided a final assessment of the experiences of a representative sample of Family Self Sufficiency participants that enrolled in 2005 and 2006. The study also examined the relationship between participants' characteristics, Family Self Sufficiency programmatic features, and program outcomes. The study found that after 4 years in the Family Self Sufficiency program, 24 percent of the study participants completed program requirements and graduated. When the study ended, 37 percent had left the program without graduating and 39 percent were still enrolled in the Family Self Sufficiency program. Program graduates were more likely to be employed than participants who did not graduate or who still were enrolled in the program. Program graduates also had higher incomes, both when they enrolled in the Family Self Sufficiency program and when they completed the program, than participants with other outcomes. Staying employed and increasing their earned incomes helped graduates to accumulate substantial savings in the

Family Self Sufficiency escrow account. The average escrow account balance was $5,294 for program graduates, representing about 27 percent of their average household income at the time of program enrollment.

State and Local Government Agencies and Nonprofits Have Also Developed an Array of Programs for Lower-Income Households to Promote Savings

Recognizing that financial literacy or education is only part of the solution to help lower-income households achieve financial security, state and local government agencies and nonprofits have developed a variety of programs targeting specific populations or serving a specific savings purpose. These include retirement savings programs, prize-linked savings programs, short-term emergency savings programs, and various asset building (or asset accumulation) programs that promote savings for specific goals (e.g., post-secondary education, home ownership, or business ownership).

Prize-Linked Savings

Several states have created prize-linked savings programs to offer a new way to help lower-income and other individuals to save. As of 2015, Michigan, Nebraska, North Carolina, and Washington have created Save to Win programs, in which participating credit unions offer their members the opportunity to open prized-linked savings accounts. A Save to Win account is designed as a 12-month share certificate that allows for unlimited deposits throughout the year. Savers are required to deposit only $25 to open an account and earn raffle tickets for every additional $25 deposited in the account, with a cap on the number of entries per month. The cap helps ensure that individuals who cannot save as much still have opportunities to win. Raffle tickets qualify participants for the chance to win monthly cash prizes and grand prizes at the end of the year. According to Doorways to Dreams Fund, since the launch of Save to Win in 2009, over 50,000 accounts have been opened with over $94 million in savings in Michigan. Moreover, the nonprofit reported that among surveyed Save to Win accountholders, between 62 percent 81 percent were financially vulnerable. Michigan passed a law in 2003 to allow for credit unions to offer "savings promotion raffles."[33] The other four states also have modified their laws to allow credit unions to offer prize-linked accounts, savings promotion raffles, or other promotional contests of chance. On the federal level, in 2014, Congress passed the American

Savings Promotion Act to provide for the use of savings promotion raffle products by financial institutions to encourage savings.[34]

Short-Term Emergency Savings

According to some nonprofit officials and academics we interviewed, federal and state savings programs primarily promote and provide tax incentives for retirement savings, which tend to benefit higher-income households more than lower-income households. At the same time, they told us that short-term or emergency saving tends to be more important for lower-income households, because it helps households meet their immediate needs—for example, to cover unexpected car repairs, medical expenses, or temporary unemployment. Some government entities and nonprofit organizations have developed pilot and other programs to promote short-term emergency savings.

- According to program officials, the AutoSave Pilot was a joint initiative of two nonprofits—New America and MDRC. Program officials told us that the pilot tested the feasibility of establishing automatic savings programs that use direct deposit to divert a small amount of after-tax wages into savings accounts. Automatic savings programs would be especially valuable for individuals who have few liquid assets and limited access to low-cost credit products, because these savings can be used as a personal safety net in the event of unanticipated expenses or a sudden decrease in income, according to New America and MDRC. AutoSave investigated two different program designs. The first program design, implemented in fall 2009, was the "opt -in program," where employees signed up for the AutoSave savings program through their employer. Employees who did not have a savings account were able to open one through a bank or credit union that partnered with the workplace site. With this version of the program design, only the savings deposits were automatic.

  The opt-in AutoSave program design had been offered to employees at eight workplace sites, ranging in size between 13 and 25,000 employees. The pilot had a special focus on generating participation among low- to moderate-income workers, although all employees were eligible to sign up. Overall participation rates ranged between 2 percent and 62 percent of all employees at these targeted workplaces, with most sites ranging between 9 percent and 25 percent. In sites where wages were tracked, the majority of participants had wage levels within the lower three-fifths of the wage distribution in their workplace. These participation results were consistent with expectations for the opt-in program design. The second investigated program design was an "opt-out program," where all employees would have been automatically enrolled in the AutoSave savings program unless they elected not to be in the program. With this design, both enrollment and deposits would have been automatic. Opt-out enrollment was not actually piloted because MDRC's assessment of the legal and operational risks concluded that while this approach would presumably be legal in some states, a lack of regulations or case law addressing the model meant that employers would be taking undue risks to implement the opt-out model. In the absence of such guidance or precedence, MDRC has determined that it is not currently feasible to implement the opt-out enrollment program design (even by using a payroll card with an attached savings product).

- According to an official at the City of San Francisco, the EARN Starter Account program, developed by the California non-profit EARN, seeks to increase the supply of starter account products that allow unbanked lower-income households to begin saving. Program participants must make at or below 50 percent of their area median income. The EARN Starter Account is an online program that rewards participants for consistently saving at least $20 each month for six months, and participants earn a maximum of $55 in matched funds over the six month period according to the nonprofit. Participants link their existing savings accounts to the EARN Starter Account platform to facilitate savings. If participants make any withdrawals over the 6 months matched funds earned will be forfeited and the account may be closed. At the end of 6 months, participants can claim the funds. Participants can continue using the EARN website for another 6 months. Since 2002, 6,000 EARN clients have saved $6.8 million dollars, and 83 percent of participants have continued to save after their formal program ended, according to a qualitative study by the nonprofit.[35] The study found that consistent savers also demonstrated a shift toward future orientation. More specifically, these program participants were planning to acquire more assets (such as further education, the purchase of a home, or founding or developing a small business). EARN is partnering with the City and County of San Francisco to bring the Starter Account platform to low-income San

Franciscans, beginning with a pilot program for public housing residents.

Some government entities and nonprofit organizations have developed programs to encourage lower-income households to save part of their income tax refund.

- According to officials at the Center for Social Development at Washington University in St. Louis, Refund to Savings is a pilot program intended to help lower-income households build savings and increase financial security.[36] Launched in 2012, the pilot is a collaboration among Washington University in St. Louis, Duke University, and Intuit Inc. According to program officials, the program is implemented through a version of Intuit's tax preparation software that is available for free to lower-income taxpayers and reaches approximately 1.2 million households. The goal of the initiative is to design and test a low-cost scalable intervention that can lead tax filers to save part of their tax refund. Under the pilot, Intuit users are assigned randomly to a treatment or control group. The treatment group uses a version of the software in which they receive prompts to motivate them to save part of their tax refund as emergency savings. In 2013, the pilot tested automatic refund splitting in which the software automatically put part of the tax filer's refund in a savings account or savings bond. According to officials at the Center for Social Development, tax filers who did not want to split their refund had to select an "I don't need to save" button to opt out. In 2013, almost 900,000 low- and moderate-income tax filers participated in the pilot, depositing approximately $5.9 million more in savings accounts than they would have without the intervention, according to the Center for Social Development officials. Data generated by program use and refund allocation behavior will be evaluated to determine whether the prompts, saving opportunity, or both increased saving levels compared with the control group, according to the Center for Social Development at Washington University.
- According to officials at MDRC and New York City's Office of Financial Empowerment, the SaveUSA program (formerly $aveNYC) is administered by the Mayor's Fund to Advance New York City and the New York City Center for Economic Opportunity and offers

lower-income households an incentive to save a portion of their tax refund.[37] According to program officials, SaveUSA was launched in 2011 in four cities (New York City, Tulsa, San Antonio, and Newark). Participants open a SaveUSA account when they file their taxes. They are required to save at least $200 of their refund for a year, and earn 50 cents for every dollar saved, with a maximum match of $500. According to an April 2014 study of the program by MDRC, nearly two-thirds of SaveUSA participants in 2011 (the program's first year) qualified for the savings match and received, on average, $191 in savings match dollars.[38] In the second program year, 39 percent of the 2011 SaveUSA sample participated again, and about 27 percent received a savings match according to the MDRC study. The MDRC study found that on average, SaveUSA group members received $96 in savings match dollars in the program's second year. According to the MDRC study, those who received a savings match in both years appear to have been in a better position to save—they tended to be older, were more likely to have more income, and were more likely to have pledged the maximum amount allowed of $1,000, compared with other SaveUSA group members. In contrast, SaveUSA group members who had especially low incomes or who pledged the minimum amount of $200 were the least likely to ever receive a savings match.

Asset-Building

Asset building is based on strategies that help households build financial or tangible assets, such as savings, a home, or a business. A number of nonprofits, states, and municipalities have developed programs to help lower-income households build assets through the use of individual development accounts or child development accounts.

As discussed, the Office of Community Services at the Administration for Children and Families administers the Assets for Independence program, which awards grants to community-based entities, nonprofits, and government agencies to implement special-purpose, matched savings accounts or individual development accounts. The length of the program, amount of matching dollars provided, allowable uses for savings, and other rules may be different from one program to the next.

An example of an individual development account is the Assets for All Alliance program. According to officials at the Opportunity Fund, this individual development account was launched in 1999 by the Opportunity

Fund (formerly Lenders for Community Development) in collaboration with the Silicon Valley Community Foundation Center for Venture Philanthropy and several community partners, including a number of nonprofit social service agencies.[39] According to a study published by the Silicon Valley Community Foundation and Lenders for Community Development, the Assets for All Alliance individual development account program is intended to help lower-income families "learn financial management skills and build assets that would help them permanently improve their economic situation."[40] Savings by program participants are "matched by philanthropic and government dollars on a two-to-one basis" according to the study. According to the Opportunity Fund, this program has resulted in 1,028 individual development accounts and $2.77 million in total savings towards asset goals.

According to officials at the Center for Social Development at Washington University in St. Louis, child development accounts are savings or investment accounts opened as early as birth. The goal of child development accounts is to promote saving and asset building for lifelong development. Child development accounts assets may be used for postsecondary education, homeownership, or enterprise development. In many cases, public and private entities deposit funds into these accounts to supplement savings for the child. Although the goal of child development accounts is long-term savings accumulation, programs differ in design and features. According to the Center for Social Development, enrollment in some states, including Maine and Nevada, is automatic unless parents opt out (opt-out programs). Some other child development accounts are voluntary or opt-in, meaning that parents must enroll their children, often by opening a 529 or bank savings account. For example, the Nevada College Kick Start program automatically deposits $50 into a 529 account for every public school kindergartner in the state according to officials at the Center for Social Development. In 2014, 70,000 students had been enrolled in Kick Start. Officials told us that Maine's College Challenge is the only statewide universal child development account program in the nation, benefiting all children born in Maine (more than 40,000 children in 2014). The program automatically deposits $500 into a 529 account on the child's behalf.

Both Nevada and Maine's 529 plans offer savings matches to state residents according to officials at the Center for Social Development. Other examples of child development accounts include those developed by national nonprofits including the Corporation for Enterprise Development and New America. According to New America, some municipalities also have launched their own child development account programs. For example, as New America reports, in San Francisco the Kindergarten to College program was launched in 2011 and opens accounts for every kindergartner in the city's public schools

CONCLUSION

Lower income households face a variety of challenges to saving. U.S. savings bonds continue to provide Americans, including those with lower-incomes, with an affordable, safe, and convenient way to save and invest. However, when Treasury ended the over-the-counter sale of paper savings bonds through financial institutions in January 2012, it created challenges for some bond buyers who had to rely on accessing TreasuryDirect to purchase savings bonds online. Treasury has taken steps to develop a more flexible and responsive Internet-based system than TreasuryDirect, but the TRIM system is in the early stages of development. Treasury intends for these changes to address some of the existing access and other challenges associated with TreasuryDirect. Currently, the Tax Time Savings Bond program provides the only means by which individuals can purchase paper savings bonds, but the program's future is uncertain, because Treasury may discontinue the program when TRIM is implemented. However, the TRIM system still will require Internet access by computer or mobile device, and Tax Time program users who lack Internet access may not be able to save by buying savings bonds at tax time if the program is discontinued. How the benefits and costs of the Tax Time program would compare when Treasury implements TRIM is not known—in part because Treasury generally has considered the program's benefits but not the program's costs. Without considering both, Treasury cannot make a fully informed decision on whether to discontinue the Tax Time program when an electronic alternative is available.

RECOMMENDATION FOR EXECUTIVE ACTION

To help ensure that Treasury can make a fully informed decision on whether to discontinue the Tax Time Savings Bond program as it implements the TRIM system, GAO recommends that the Secretary of the Treasury consider the benefits and costs of the Tax Time program in future decisions on whether to extend the program.

AGENCY COMMENTS

We provided a draft of this report to Treasury and IRS for review and comment. In their comment letter, Treasury agreed with GAO's recommendation and stated that it would conduct a cost-benefit analysis of the Tax Time Savings Bonds program. Treasury also provided technical comments, which we incorporated, as appropriate. We also provided draft excerpts for technical comment to federal and other agencies—including the Departments of Health and Human Services and Housing and Urban Development, FDIC, New York City's Office of Financial Empowerment, and San Francisco Office of Financial Empowerment—and nonprofit organizations, including the Center for Social Development at Washington University, Doorways to Dreams Fund, MDRC, and Opportunity Fund. These third parties provided technical comments, which we have incorporated, as appropriate.

Cindy Brown Barnes
Director
Education, Workforce, and Income Security

APPENDIX I: OBJECTIVES, SCOPE, AND METHODOLOGY

Our review examines (1) the effect of Treasury's elimination of paper U.S. savings bonds, including on the savings bond program and bond purchases; (2) the extent to which Treasury's Tax Time Savings Bond program has promoted savings, particularly by lower-income households, and Treasury's plans for the program's future; and (3) the extent to which lower-income households are saving using financial products, and some of the government and nonprofit programs developed to promote savings by lower-income households.

For all three objectives, we analyzed various data. First, we used data issued by the Department of the Treasury (Treasury) on the amount of U.S. savings bonds purchased from 2001 through 2013 to analyze trends in savings bond purchases over this period, including the effect of the Treasury's elimination of paper savings bonds on savings bond purchases. Second, we used data from the triennial Survey of Consumer Finances (SCF) issued by the Board of Governors of the Federal Reserve System for survey years 2001, 2004, 2007, 2010, and 2013 to estimate the percentage of U.S. households holding financial assets, including U.S. savings bonds; the median value of such financial assets held by U.S. households, and the median income of households. The survey data include information on families' balance sheets, pensions, income, investments, and demographic characteristics. We analyzed the U.S. population data as a whole and also considered the bottom two income quintiles separately. We chose these survey years because they provide a period of about 10 years prior to and 1 year after the discontinuation of the sale of paper savings bonds at financial institutions. We analyzed the U.S. population data as a whole and also considered the bottom two income quintiles separately. SCF data are based on probability samples and estimates are formed using the appropriate estimation weights provided with the survey's data. Because each of these samples follows a probability procedure based on random selections, they represent only one of a large number of samples that could have been drawn. Since each sample could have provided different estimates, we express our confidence in the precision of our particular sample's results as a 95 percent confidence interval (i.e., plus or minus 2.5 percentage points). This is the interval that would contain the actual population value for 95 percent of the samples we could have drawn. Unless otherwise noted, all percentage estimates have 95 percent confidence intervals that are within 5 percentage points of the estimate itself, and all numerical estimates other than percentages have 95 percent confidence intervals that are within 5 percent of the estimate itself. We also reviewed documentation on the SCF, such as codebooks and Federal Reserve bulletins. Third, we used aggregated data provided by the Internal Revenue Service (IRS) on income tax filers who used at least part of their tax refunds to buy paper savings bonds from 2010 through 2013 to analyze the number of tax filers who bought paper savings bonds, including those with adjusted gross incomes of $25,000 or below—the lowest income category reported in the data—and the amount of savings bonds they purchased.[1] We also used the aggregated data to analyze refund options used by the tax filers (such as paper check and paper savings bond, direct deposit and paper savings bond, or paper savings bond only) and demographic information about the filers, such as their age. We assessed the reliability of the data we used by interviewing knowledgeable officials, and conducting manual testing on relevant data fields, such as the number of tax filers who participated in the program and amounts of savings bonds purchased. We found the data we reviewed to be sufficiently reliable for the purposes of our analyses.

To examine the effect of Treasury's elimination of paper U.S. savings bond, including on the savings bond program and bond purchases, we reviewed data on savings bonds purchases from 2001 through 2013, and analyzed trends in purchases for this time period, including before and after paper savings bonds were discontinued in January 2012. Specifically, to analyze long- term trends in savings bond purchases and more recent trends since the end of paper sales, we estimated two econometric models. The first model was based on a portfolio choice model, and modeled purchases as a function of interest rates, inflation, and economy-wide risk (using the Chicago Board Options Exchange's Volatility Index). In other words, consumers may make savings bond purchase decisions the same way they make other decisions about financial portfolio allocation, based on risk and return considerations. The second model was based on linear and quadratic time trends to capture the long-term reduction in purchases. We included monthly seasonal effects in both models. The drop in savings bond purchases after the end of paper sales was consistent with long-term trends and generally not statistically significant. The drop in purchases after the end of paper sales also was consistent with the reduction in interest rates at the time (the coefficient on interest rates was highly statistically significant). As with any econometric model, our approach is imperfect and is unlikely to include all factors that influence savings bond purchases. Additional data over time might provide different or more definitive estimates of the change in purchases associated with the end of paper sales. We reviewed Federal Register releases on TreasuryDirect and its replacement system, the Treasury Retail Investment Manager; Treasury documentation, including a description of data in the monthly statement of public debt, estimates of cost savings from eliminating paper savings bonds, press releases, Bureau of the Fiscal Service's President's budgets and capital investment plans; and TreasuryDirect materials. To assess the reliability of Treasury's cost estimates, we interviewed Treasury officials on how the estimates were determined and reported. We also interviewed Treasury officials to discuss a range of issues related to its savings bond program, including the benefits and costs of eliminating paper savings bonds, concerns raised about TreasuryDirect, and plans for replacing TreasuryDirect.

To determine the extent to which Treasury's Tax Time Savings Bond program has promoted savings, we analyzed IRS data on the use of the program by tax filers for tax years 2010 through 2013 (as discussed in detail above). We also reviewed IRS documentation on the program, such as descriptions on how the program operates and answers to common questions about the program, and studies on the Tax Time program published by academics and nonprofit organizations focusing on social or economic policy. We interviewed Treasury and IRS officials about the Tax Time program's operations, benefits, costs, and future in terms of its expiration.

To better understand the extent to which this program can help lower-income households to save, we interviewed nonprofit organizations focusing on social or economic policy, including Doorways to Dreams Fund, New America, Corporation for Enterprise Development, and MDRC.

To examine the extent to which lower-income households are saving using financial products, we examined SCF data for survey years 2001, 2004, 2007, 2010, and 2013 (as described in greater detail above). Based on these data, we defined lower-income households as the lower two distributions (or quintiles) of households in the United States.[2] To describe some of the government and nonprofit programs developed to promote savings by lower-income households, we conducted Internet and literature searches for research, initiatives, testimonies, and studies on savings programs targeting lower-income households and reviewed materials on such programs. We specifically reviewed select federal, state, local, and nonprofit programs targeting either long-term (such as retirement or asset accumulation) or short-term savings goals for lower-income households. For the purposes of this report, we focused on programs designed to promote savings using financial assets, such as bank accounts, bonds, mutual funds, and retirement accounts. We generally excluded programs designed to promote savings through home ownership or other nonfinancial assets. For federal programs, we focused our review on federal agencies involved in promoting financial literacy that are members of the multiagency Financial Literacy and Education Commission (FLEC). We interviewed six FLEC member agencies—the Departments of the Treasury, Housing and Urban Development, Health and Human Services, and Education; the Federal Deposit Insurance Corporation; and the Bureau of Consumer Financial Protection, also known as the Consumer Financial Protection Bureau—about their savings programs and reviewed related documentation.

We also reviewed select state, local, and nonprofit programs targeting lower-income households. We selected these programs based on our research of savings programs for lower-income households and interviews with FLEC members and other stakeholders. For the programs we selected, we interviewed relevant program officials and reviewed documentation on the programs, including information on participation in the programs where available. Finally, we interviewed other relevant stakeholders, including Doorways to Dreams Fund, New America, Corporation for Enterprise Development, MDRC, Consumers for Paper Options, and academics.

We conducted this performance audit from August 2014 to July 2015 in accordance with generally accepted government auditing standards. Those standards require that we plan and perform the audit to obtain sufficient, appropriate evidence to provide a reasonable basis for our findings and conclusions based on our audit objectives. We believe that the evidence obtained provides a reasonable basis for our findings and conclusions based on our audit objectives.

End Notes

[1] The Federal Reserve Board's SCF is a triennial cross-sectional survey of families in the United States. The survey data include information on families' balance sheets, pensions, income, investments, and demographic characteristics. The most recent survey was conducted in 2013. For purposes of this report, we define lower-income households in the context of SCF data as those households whose income falls in the bottom 40 percent. The range of income for this category of households in the latest survey conducted in 2013 was from $0 to $36,523 and the average household income was about $21,000.

[2] The Financial Literacy and Education Commission was created in 2003 as a multiagency commission to coordinate among federal agencies and between federal agencies and state, local, nonprofit, and private entities related to financial literacy initiatives. Twenty-two federal entities are members of the commission, with the Treasury Secretary serving as the chair and Consumer Financial Protection Bureau Director serving as the vice chair.

[3] Most of the securities that Treasury issues to the public are marketable, meaning that once the government issues them they can be resold by whoever owns them. Marketable debt consists of bills, notes, and bonds. Currently, Treasury issues bills with maturities ranging from a few days to 52 weeks; notes with maturities of 2, 3, 5, 7, and 10 years; bonds that mature in 30 years; Treasury Inflation-Protected Securities with maturities of 5, 10, and 30 years; and Floating Rate Notes that mature in 2 years.

[4] For Series EE bonds, issued since May 2005, the interest rate is determined by taking the market yields of the 10-year Treasury Note and adjusting that by the value of components unique to savings bonds, including options that permit early redemption (redemption after the first 12 months) and tax deferral.

[5] The number of funded TreasuryDirect accounts is a snapshot of the number of accounts containing one or more savings bonds or marketable securities on a particular date.

[6] We adjusted the monthly savings bonds purchased for inflation using the consumer price index, with June 2014 as the base month, before aggregating purchases by year.

[7] In 2001, the 95 percent confidence interval on median savings bonds held, conditional on holding any, was $1,226 to $1,401. In 2013, it was $817 to $1,183.

[8] Households earning less than $25,000 were the lowest household income category for which Census data were reported on computer and Internet usage.

[9] FDIC, 2013 FDIC National Survey of Unbanked and Underbanked Households (Washington, D.C.: October 2014).

[10] The number of funded TreasuryDirect accounts is a snapshot of the number of accounts containing one or more savings bonds or marketable securities on a particular date. The date for this snapshot is December 31, 2011, which was just before Treasury discontinued the sale of paper savings bonds in January 2012.

[11] Proposed Collection of Information: TreasuryDirect System, 79 Fed. Reg. 44,491 (July 31, 2014).

[12] IRS Tax Form 8888 Allocation of Refund (Including Savings Bond Purchases) allows tax filers to directly deposit their refund to either two or three accounts at a bank or other financial institution (such as a mutual fund, brokerage firm, or credit union) in the United States, and to use at least part of the refund to purchase up to $5,000 in Series I paper savings bonds.

[13] We calculated the total number of tax filers using the Tax Time program by aggregating IRS data on the total number of tax returns filed for tax years 2010 through 2013, for a total of 142,119. Since about 20 percent of tax filers participated in the program in more than 1 year, the number of unique tax filers is less than this amount.

[14] The Earned Income Tax Credit was first enacted by the Tax Reduction Act of 1975, Pub. L. No. 94-12, § 204(a), 89 Stat. 26, 30 (1975) (codified as amended at 26 U.S.C. § 32).

[15] According to Treasury officials, if Treasury were to discontinue the Tax Time program, tax filers would still have the option of having their tax refund deposited into their TreasuryDirect account through which they could then purchase electronic savings bonds. Expiration of the program would only eliminate the availability of paper savings bonds, but not the ability to use a tax refund to purchase electronic savings bonds.

[16] GAO, Cost Estimating and Assessment Guide: Best Practices for Developing and Managing Capital Program Costs, GAO-09-3SP (Washington, D.C.: March 2009).

[17] Our report focuses primarily on programs that promote savings or asset-building through financial assets, such as bank accounts, savings bonds, mutual funds, and retirement funds. As a result, we generally excluded programs that promote savings or asset-building through home purchases or other nonfinancial assets.

[18] Financial assets in SCF include bank accounts, certificates of deposit, savings bonds, bonds, stocks, mutual funds, retirement accounts, and cash value life insurance.

[19] The 95 percent confidence interval on median income was $13,227 to $15,180 for the lowest quintile and $27,734 to $29,080 for the next quintile.

[20] The mean, inflation-adjusted non-retirement financial assets of the whole population were down between 2001 and 2013 because of a decline in the median and in the holdings of the 25th, 75th, 90th, and 95th percentiles of the population. The mean and the 75th, 90th, 95th, and 99th percentiles values of retirement savings for the population as a whole increased between 2001 and 2013, and this growth in retirement assets helped drive slight growth in mean total financial assets for the population as a whole.

[21] In the 2013 survey, underbanked households are those that have a bank account and have used at least one of the following alternative financial services from non-bank providers in the last 12 months: money orders, check cashing, remittances, payday loans, refund anticipation loans, rent-to-own services, pawn shops loans, or auto title loans.

[22] See GAO, Financial Literacy: Overlap of Programs Suggest There May Be Opportunities for Consolidation, GAO-12-588 (Washington, D.C.: July 23, 2012).

[23] States recognize that many of their residents currently lack access to retirement savings plans through their private sector employers and there are efforts in a number of states to study or create retirement savings plans for their residents. GAO is currently conducting a more detailed review of state efforts to increase private sector coverage in retirement savings programs and that report is forthcoming (GAO-15-556).

[24] A myRA is subject to Roth IRA annual income eligibility limits—which means that people who have an annual income of less than $129,000 for individuals and $191,000 for couples can participate. These limits are subject to annual cost-of-living adjustments. Each

individual saver, not the employer, will be responsible for complying with these income limits.

[25] According to FDIC, FDIC, in collaboration with CFPB, offers a stand-alone instructor-led module targeting the needs of older adults (age 62 and older). FDIC in collaboration with the Small Business Administration offers an instructor-led curriculum focusing on the needs of new or existing entrepreneurs. FDIC also offers Money Smart for Young People which offers curriculums to promote financial understanding in preschool to high school aged children.

[26] FDIC, A Longitudinal Evaluation of the Intermediate-term Impact of the Money Smart Financial Education Curriculum Upon Consumers' Behavior and Confidence (April 2007).

[27] FDIC, Model Safe Accounts Pilot: Final Report (April 2012).

[28] The Assets for Independence Act was passed in 1998, but Administration for Children and Families began awarding grants in 1999. Pub. L. No. 105-285, Tit. IV, 112 Stat. 2702, 2759 (1998) (codified as amended at 42 U.S.C. § 604 note).

[29] Participants also are permitted to transfer their IDA savings to support the asset goal of an account-holding spouse or dependent.

[30] In fiscal year 2015, the program was made available to families participating in the Section 8 Project-Based Rental Assistance program.

[31] The activities in this account were previously funded as a set-aside in the Tenant-Based Rental Assistance Administrative Fee and as part of the Resident Opportunity and Self-Sufficiency set-aside in the Public Housing Capital Fund accounts; in fiscal year 2013, those programs were funded at $56.8 and $18 million, respectively.

[32] HUD, Evaluation of the Family Self-Sufficiency Program: Prospective Study (February 2011). In 2004, HUD contracted with Planmatics, Inc., and Abt Associates Inc. to design and implement the study. The team selected a representative sample of 100 public housing authorities in the first year and collected information from FSS coordinators in 2005.

[33] 2003 Mich. Pub. Acts 215, § 411 (codified at Mich. Comp. Laws § 490.411). 34American Savings Promotion Act, Pub. L. No. 113-251, 128 Stat. 2888 (2014).

[35] EARN, What Motivates Low Income Workers to Save Money (January: 2010). According to the report, EARN identified a group of 218 alumni who have successfully completed its program and used their funds. A total of 126 alumni were contacted for interviews, with thirty of them agreeing to be interviewed by phone or in person. EARN developed an interview script and protocol used for both phone and in-person interviews that explored a wide range of topics about the participant's asset accumulation patterns and perceptions before, during, and after the individual development account program. EARN expects to continue these interviews over time to build a large and growing sample.

[36] Center for Social Development, Washington University in St, Louis, Refund to Savings (R2S): Insight from the Field, 2012 (St. Louis, MO: 2013).

[37] According to a 2014 MDRC study, in January 2011, enrollment in the SaveUSA study began in select Volunteer Income Tax Assistance sites in New York City, Tulsa, Newark, and San Antonio. In addition to providing tax return preparation services to hundreds of clients per week, Volunteer Income Tax Assistance staff marketed the SaveUSA account, enrolled individuals in the study, and helped SaveUSA group members open their SaveUSA account. The program was voluntary, but anyone meeting the program's eligibility requirements and interested in opening a SaveUSA account had to agree to participate in the study to be eligible to open an account. The Volunteer Income Tax Assistance sites recruited about 2,500 individuals into the study between January and April 2011, the 2010 tax return preparation season.

[38] Gilda Azurdia, Stephen Freedman, Gaye Hamilton, and Caroline Schultz, Encouraging Low- and Moderate-Income Tax Filers to Save: Implementation and Interim Impact Findings from the SaveUSA Evaluation (New York, NY: April 2014).

[39] Silicon Valley Community Foundation and Lenders for Community Development, Families Saving and Building Hope: 2007 Report on Graduates of the Assets for All Alliances (Mountain View, CA).

[40] Silicon Valley Community Foundation and Lenders for Community Development, 2007 Report, 3.

End Notes for Appendix I

[1] For tax year 2010, IRS only had data on the amount of paper savings bonds tax filers asked to be purchase and not the actual purchase figures. IRS officials explained that in almost all cases, the requests go through and are processed for the exact amount requested.

[2] For a given characteristic, a percentile can be used to define a family's rank relative to other families—when a distribution is divided at every 20th percentile, as in the SCF data, the groups are known as quintiles.

In: U.S. Savings Bonds, Municipal Bonds … ISBN: 978-1-63484-698-1
Editor: Henrietta Walters

Chapter 2

THE DEMAND FOR MUNICIPAL BONDS: ISSUES FOR CONGRESS*

Darryl E. Getter and Raj Gnanarajah

SUMMARY

Municipal bonds are debt securities issued by states, cities, counties, and other government-created agencies to finance capital projects, such as highways, airports, sewers, bridges, schools, hospitals, and other public goods for residents. The municipal bond market is large and varied, consisting of more than an estimated 1.5 million bond types and more than an estimated 55,000 issuers borrowing to finance a variety of civic projects. The U.S. municipal bond market had a total of $3.7 trillion outstanding issuances by year end 2014, reflecting a 3.2% decline from its peak in 2010.

Meanwhile, the outstanding municipal debt associated with financing of capital projects has risen over the last decade. The distressed financial situation of the Commonwealth of Puerto Rico, while not the primary focus of this report, serves as an example of financial distress attributed to an increase in longer-term liabilities. Rising indebtedness levels may have led some municipal bond issuers to curtail new issuances rather than further increase longer-term liabilities.

* This is an edited, reformatted and augmented version of a Congressional Research Service publication R44146, prepared for Members and Committees of Congress, dated August 14, 2015.

Various bills that would impact the municipal bond market have been introduced in the 114th Congress.

- The Move America Act of 2015, S. 1186, would create expanded tax incentives for infrastructure projects.
- The Municipal Bond Market Support Act of 2015, H.R. 2229, would increase the annual municipal debt limit that could be exempt from $10 million to $30 million on the amount of tax-exempt obligations a small issuer may issue for a bank to purchase.

In addition, legislation has been introduced to protect taxpayers at the federal level from municipal bond defaults.

- The No Taxpayer Bailouts for Unsustainable State and Local Pensions Act, H.R. 1476, for example, would prohibit the Secretary of the Treasury and the Board of Governors of the Federal Reserve System from providing any financial assistance to state and local government pension plan funds.

Congress generally has supported policies to encourage credit access for state and local public-sector entities. This report informs Congress about various developments related to the demand for municipal bonds. Beginning with investor holding trends, the household share of municipal bondholders has decreased whereas the share of various financial intermediaries holding municipals, particularly depository banking institutions, has increased. Changes in the composition of investors could be related to several types of financial risks (e.g., interest rate, liquidity, default). Likewise, various regulatory developments also influence the profitability of municipal bonds for different bondholder types, and thus their willingness to hold these securities. This report also presents concerns expressed by the Securities and Exchange Commission (SEC) regarding the need for improved disclosures to inform investors about the financial health of municipal issuers and consistent accounting practices.

INTRODUCTION

A municipal bond is a debt security issued by states, cities, counties, and other government-created entities to pay for capital projects, such as highways, airports, sewers, bridges, schools, hospitals, and other infrastructure expenditures. Municipal bond issuers include state and local municipal governments as well as other municipal entities (e.g., utilities, water districts, hospital authorities), and there are more than 55,000 issuers of municipal bonds.[1] The estimate of more than 1.5 million different types of municipal bonds reflects the wide and diverse range of civic projects that are financed in this market.[2] Municipal bonds are also distinguished from other types of bonds (e.g., corporate, U.S. Treasuries) by the tax treatment for individuals. The interest on municipals is generally exempt from federal taxes. Residents who invest in their state or local municipality bonds may also have the interest on these bonds exempt from state or local taxes.[3]

The Municipal Securities Rulemaking Board (MSRB), an independent rulemaking entity established by Congress, provides oversight of the municipal bond markets and participants. The MSRB was created by the Securities Act Amendments of 1975.[4] MSRB is considered to be a self-regulatory organization (SRO), and its rules are approved by the Securities and Exchange Commission (SEC) and enforced primarily by the Financial Industry Regulatory Authority (FINRA), which is another SRO. SROs are subject to SEC oversight and primarily regulate broker-dealers, who earn fees for trading in securities markets.[5] All municipal broker-dealers as well as municipal advisors, who earn fees for advisory services, must register with the MSRB.[6] Generally speaking, the main objective of the MSRB is to promote fairness and transparency in the municipal securities markets.

Following the 2007-2009 recession, state and local public-sector entities have encountered rising fiscal gaps as well as rising indebted levels associated with the financing of long-term capital projects, and thus more distressed financial situations.[7] While fiscal gaps may be narrowed by reducing spending and raising taxes, the proceeds generated by municipal bond issuances are typically designated for the funding of longer-term capital projects. All forms of lending, however, are risky, and bondholders face a range of financial risks. Proper disclosure of risk allows investors to determine whether they want to lend and how much of their funds they may be willing to lose in the event the borrower is unable to repay. In addition to the customary risk and return trade-off assessment, financial intermediaries (e.g., banks, credit unions, insurance companies) are also faced with additional regulations affecting the cost and, therefore, the return on municipal bond investments.

This report examines various influences on investors' demand for municipal bonds, with a particular focus on financial institutions; it also discusses policy issues for Congress. The report presents some recent investor holding trends, followed by an overview of various types of financial risks associated with municipal bond investments. In light of the financial risks, it discusses the challenges associated with improved financial disclosures of municipal bonds. Finally, depository banks that choose to hold municipal bonds face added regulatory requirements, which are also discussed given that banks may both lend and facilitate lending in this market. The *Appendix* provides an overview of the fiscal health of state and local municipal issuers since the 2007-2009 recession.

Financial Intermediaries: Institutions and Markets

Financial intermediation is the process of matching borrowers with lenders (i.e., savers). Depository intermediaries, such as banks and credit unions, for example, generally acquire funds from lenders (in the form of checking and savings deposits) and subsequently make loans to borrowers. The aggregate returns from lending activities are distributed between the intermediary (that keeps the loans in its asset portfolio) and the savers (that maintain deposits in the lending institution). Alternatively, financial intermediation may be conducted via the bond and asset-backed securities markets. Bonds are conceptually equivalent to loans. Investors assume the role of lenders when they purchase bonds from issuers, who are essentially borrowing the investment funds.[8] Similarly, investors that purchase financial interests in an asset-backed security, which is created by transforming a pool of numerous bonds into tranches (i.e., sets of tiered payment structures prescribing the sequence that investors are to be repaid and associated investment yields), jointly act as lenders to the underlying pool of borrowers. Financial intermediation activities that occur in the financial markets (rather than facilitated by depository institutions) may be referred to as *shadow banking* activities. All forms of financial intermediation bear the typical risks (e.g., asset market, liquidity, default, systemic) associated with lending.[9]

TRENDS IN MUNICIPAL BOND HOLDINGS FOLLOWING THE 2007-2009 RECESSION

Figure 1 shows that the outstanding issuances in the municipal bond market, as reported by the Federal Reserve, totaled $3.65 trillion in 2014, down from a $3.77 trillion peak in 2010.[10] The municipal bond market grew in size by 24.9% from 2005 to 2010, but decreased by 3.2% from 2010 to 2014. The largest sector holding municipal bonds are household investors, which includes some nonfinancial businesses (e.g., nonprofit organizations).

Household investors reduced their market share of municipal bond holdings from 54% to 43% between 2005 and 2014.[11] Households still hold the largest share of municipals, perhaps as a result of the tax advantages for individual investors.

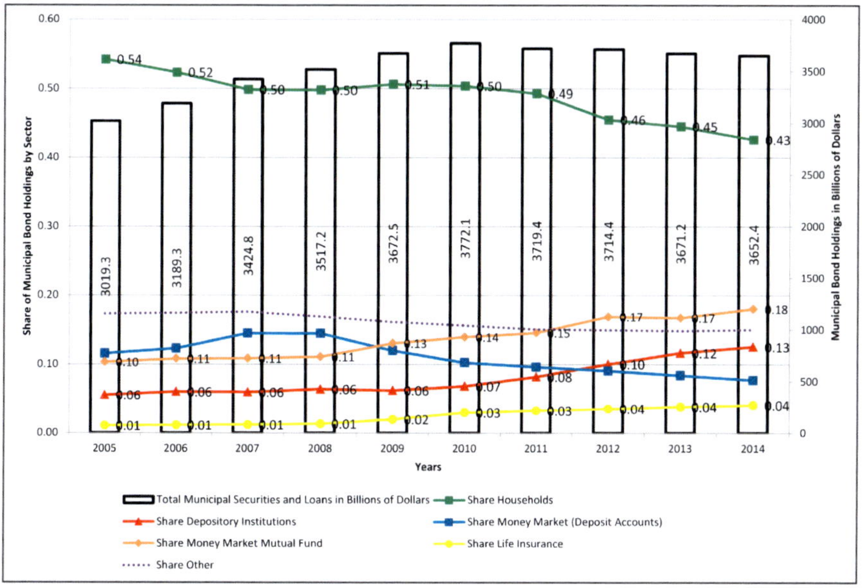

Source: Federal Reserve Flow of Funds.

Note: Congressional Research Service (CRS) Computations.

Figure 1. U.S. Municipal Bond Market: Total Outstanding and Bondholders, by Sector. (2005-2014)

Whereas the household share of municipal holdings declined, the share of municipal bonds held by other financial entities increased. *Figure 1* shows that depository institutions (i.e., banks and credit unions that maintain federally insured deposits) have more than doubled their share of holdings.[12] Life insurance companies have quadrupled their share of holdings from 1% to 4%. As the share of municipal bonds held via money market deposit accounts fell since 2005, the share held via money market mutual funds rose.[13] More time may be needed to determine whether the observed trends in investor composition reflect temporary or permanent shifts.

UNDERSTANDING THE FINANCIAL RISKS RELATED TO HOLDING MUNICIPAL BONDS

The willingness to hold or the demand for municipal bond investments depends upon various factors, including investor appetites for financial risks.[14] This section discusses the different types of financial risks that influence the willingness and therefore the decision to hold municipal bonds. One or more of these types of risks (discussed in no particular order) may influence investors' decisions to hold municipal bonds.[15]

Asset Market Risk

Asset market risk with respect to bond holdings may also be referred to as interest rate risk. For example, suppose a lender makes a loan to a borrower at a fixed interest rate. A rise in market interest rates on the following day reduces the present value of the loan made the day before, meaning that the lender could have earned a higher yield by waiting a day. At times when interest rates are expected to rise, the lenders may want to sell the current loan for cash and originate a new loan the next day at the higher interest rate, thus avoiding ownership of the original asset should it decline in value.

Increased interest rate risk may cause some investors to sell municipal bond holdings. When current interest rates are expected to rise relative to the agreed-upon note rate of existing bonds, the present value (price) of existing bonds will decrease relative to newly issued bonds with higher rates of return (yields). Given that interest rates have remained at historic lows, some investors may have been anxious about holding existing bonds in their portfolios in anticipation of future increases in interest rates that would reduce current bond values.

Liquidity Risk

Economists view the concept of *liquidity* from a variety of perspectives. Liquidity is a term that typically refers to how quickly an asset can be converted to cash. In the context of bond markets, liquidity pertains to how quickly an asset can be bought or sold in the marketplace. *Liquidity risk*, therefore, can refer to holding assets that cannot quickly be converted into cash to satisfy immediate needs or are traded in *thin markets* (i.e., low volume of buying and selling). Financial intermediaries typically assume liquidity risk when holding less liquid loans in their asset portfolios. If investors finance less liquid, longer-term assets (e.g., bonds) with more liquid, shorter-term obligations (e.g., demand deposits) they risk having to incur large losses if they need to liquidate some or all of those assets to repay the shorter-term obligations on time.[16]

Newly issued municipal bonds tend to be the most actively traded (primary market trading); bond trading after initial issuance, referred to as secondary market trading, declines significantly.[17] The SEC cites studies reporting that one-third of municipals trade only once after initial issuance, the remaining bonds trade only two or three times during their lifetimes, and 5% of all municipals may only trade once every 12 years.[18] Only a small amount of outstanding municipal bonds are purchased or offered for sale on a day-to-day basis, resulting in a thin secondary market for these securities.[19] Hence, municipal bonds trade in small volumes in the over-the-counter market on an irregular basis (in comparison to trading in large volumes on organized exchanges). The thin secondary market is why the municipal bonds are generally characterized as being illiquid (although some municipal bonds may be considered less illiquid relative to others).

The thin secondary market trading volume is why the prices of individual municipal securities must be estimated, which increases the probability of incurring a loss (i.e., rising liquidity risk) under circumstances in which investors unexpectedly needed to liquidate their bond holdings.[20] Prices are frequently determined by observing past trades of bonds that arguably share similar characteristics, which has become easier for individual investors in recent years as a result of the MSRB's Electronic Municipal Market Access website.[21] Consequently, some investors, particularly those anticipating their future cash flow needs, may choose to convert their municipal bonds holdings into assets in which the values do not need to be estimated and, therefore, characterized by lower levels of liquidity risk.

Default Risk

Default risk refers to the risk that borrowers (or bond issuers) will not repay all principal and interest owed or as scheduled. In light of the thousands of issues, municipal bond defaults are likely to be idiosyncratic or unique to the financial conditions tied to the locality or entity where they were issued.[22]

The default rate for municipal bonds tracked by the S&P Municipal Bond Index, for example, was 0.144% in 2012, 0.107% in 2013, and 0.17% in 2014.[23] In light of infrequent default experiences, municipals are considered to be historically safe investments.[24]

The Federal Reserve Bank of New York has found that reports by major bond rating agencies about municipal bond defaults only include rated bonds, but inclusion of the unrated portion of the market significantly increases the number of municipal default frequencies.[25] Furthermore, several state and local municipalities experienced financial distress episodes following the 2007 2009 recession. Some municipal bond issuers saw lower tax revenues and higher expenditures.[26] Some municipalities saw their credit ratings downgraded due to growing indebtedness, frequently associated with underfunded pensions.[27] Some general obligations were cut to junk (low grade, high default risk) bond status;[28] since 2008, some issuers have filed for Chapter 9 bankruptcy.[29]

When an issuer's credit rating is low, bond insurance may be purchased to help attract investors.[30] The financial guaranty insurance industry, that is, monoline (bond) insurers, provides insurance against the default risk of municipal bonds and asset-backed bond issuances. After 2007, monoline insurers experienced losses on mortgage-backed securities guarantees resulting in a loss of their AAA ratings.[31] Some investors may be less comfortable holding insured municipal bonds in light of reports about some bond insurers that are still recovering from previous financial losses.[32]

- In the 114th Congress, the No Taxpayer Bailouts for Unsustainable State and Local Pensions Act (H.R. 1476) was introduced to prohibit the Secretary of the Treasury and the Board of Governors of the Federal Reserve System from providing any financial assistance to state and local government pension plan funds. If the source of financial stress for many municipalities is related to the funding of municipal employee pensions, then this bill would prevent the federal government from acting as the ultimate guarantor for municipal investors. This bill could encourage some municipalities to apply available funds to cover pension liabilities and fund more non-pension liabilities via borrowing, thereby shifting more default risk to non-pension liabilities where it may still be possible to request federal assistance.

Systemic Risk

Bond markets, as with all financial asset markets, are also vulnerable to *systemic risk* crises. A systemic risk crisis can occur in the municipal bond market when bondholders suddenly lose confidence (or panic) about the likelihood of repayment and simultaneously rush to sell or liquidate their municipal securities holdings.[33] Given that municipals trade infrequently and their prices are estimated, investors may not be able to obtain timely market information about changes in issuer default risk or changes in overall market perceptions of default risk. Although investors can obtain information about the risks associated with their bond holdings, (e.g., the financial statements of the bond issuers or on-site inspections of the progress of a municipal project), recurring announcements of various municipals' fiscal problems may influence bondholders' perceptions of risk exposure. Growing pessimism can suddenly manifest itself in the form of a market retrenchment—often referred to as a systemic risk *run* or *flight-to-quality* event—when investors suddenly attempt to liquidate their bond holdings before issuers become insolvent.[34]

The Financial Stability Oversight Council (FSOC), established to identify risks to the financial stability of the United States, provided an assessment in its annual report regarding the potential of a systemic risk crisis in the municipal bond market generated specifically by the debt crisis in Puerto Rico.[35] Puerto Rico has outstanding municipal debt totaling more than $70 billion, and the credit rating agencies have downgraded the issuances to junk status.[36] According to the FSOC, evidence of an erosion of investor confidence in the broader municipal bond market stemming from financial challenges idiosyncratic to Puerto Rico has not been observed. As long as investors do not consider the financial distress of one or more municipal issuers to be indicative of the broader financial health of other issuers, then it may be possible to avoid a systemic risk panic in the broader municipal securities market.

Disclosing and Evaluating Municipal Bond Risks

The Securities Act of 1933 requires full disclosure of material financial information about securities sold and granted in the securities market.[37] The federal government, however, is limited in its ability to regulate the municipal bond market even though it is a national market due to concerns associated with federal-state comity.[38] The Securities Exchange Act of 1934 created the Securities and Exchange Commission (SEC), giving it broad authority over the securities markets *with the exception of the municipal securities market*.[39] The Securities Acts Amendments of 1975, commonly referred to as the Tower Amendment to the Securities Exchange Act of 1934, prohibits the federal government from requiring

> any issuer of municipal securities, directly or indirectly through a purchaser or prospective purchaser of securities from the issuer, to file with the [Securities and Exchange] Commission or the [Municipal Securities Rulemaking] Board prior to the sale of such securities by the issuer any application, report, or document in connection with the issuance, sale, or distribution of such securities.[40]

Issuers of municipal bonds are not required to register their securities and thus are not subject to SEC disclosure requirements. The SEC does not have the authority to require state and local municipalities to follow the Generally Accepted Accounting Principles (GAAP) for state and local municipalities, established by the Governmental Accounting Standards Board (GASB).[41] Compliance with GASB rules by state and local municipalities is voluntary. Individual states can pass statutes to require compliance with GASB or other preferred accounting methods. For example, the SEC has noted that the state of New Jersey has passed a state law requiring its localities to use statutorily mandated accounting methods as opposed to a nationally recognized accounting standard, such as those issued by the GASB.[42]

Because municipal issuers do not have to meet standard SEC disclosure requirements, disclosure practices may vary by jurisdiction, state requirements, and type of security offerings (e.g., general obligation bonds, revenue bonds). Accounting practices are inconsistent across state and local governments. State definitions of budget items may vary considerably, making the ability to compare risks across municipal jurisdictions less effective.[43] Conflicts of interests that may exist between the issuer, underwriter, and other principals may not be sufficiently disclosed at an initial offering. Disclosures at new offerings may lack sufficient information about the existence of bank loans or other municipal obligations owed by the issuer. Investors may also be vulnerable to improper disclosures if municipal bond credit rating changes, particularly in municipal markets that trade infrequently. Such issues suggest that investors are unable to accurately determine how much default risk they would assume when considering municipal bond investments.

Complicating matters, bondholders may be unsure whether they rank first or last in payment priority should an issuer become insolvent.[44] In accordance with the Tenth Amendment of the U.S. Constitution, the federal government may not grant a bankruptcy petition for a municipality without permission from the state because bankruptcy is a federal process. Some 26 states allow municipalities to file for bankruptcy.[45] For states that have not enacted laws specifying whether it or its local public-sector entity can declare bankruptcy, bondholders would not know the order of payment priority in case of an asset liquidation episode, possibly prompting some of them to sell their municipal bonds. In cases where state and local courts may favor pension funds over bondholders, it becomes particularly important for bondholders to be fully aware of the repayment risks.

Meeting various disclosure standards may be considered burdensome particularly for smaller municipal issuers. For example, issuers pay standardization and transmittal requirements for data.[46] Standardization of the reporting cycle, (i.e., quarterly or monthly) may be expensive if, for example, financial statements were required to be audited and credit ratings had to be updated at each interval.[47] Generally speaking, small financial entities (e.g., community banks, credit unions, small bond issuers) typically lack the volume of transactions commensurate with the compliance costs of various industry regulations compared with their larger competitors.

Regulatory Actions to Improve Municipal Market Disclosures

The SEC has brought attention to the need to improve disclosure practices of state and local governments in light of alleged omissions of material information that investors may have found necessary to fully understand the risks associated with municipal bond investments.[48] The SEC may still enforce federal securities antifraud provisions against municipal issuers when pertinent financial information is withheld from or misrepresented to investors in violation of SEC Rule 15c2-12.[49] The SEC has suggested recommendations designed to improve transparency and liquidity in the municipal securities markets.[50]

Although federal disclosure requirements may not be imposed on municipal issuers, broker-dealers that facilitate the buying and selling of municipal bonds are regulated. The Municipal Securities Rulemaking Board was established as an independent entity in 1975 by the Tower Amendment to issue regulations and rules for the municipal bond broker-dealers. The MSRB has authority to make rules regulating the municipal securities activities of securities firms and banks that underwrite, trade, and sell municipal securities, as well as municipal advisory activities of municipal advisors. Title IX of the Dodd-Frank Wall Street Reform and Consumer Protection Act of 2010 (Dodd-Frank Act)[51] expanded the MSRB's jurisdiction, which had included broker-dealers (that earn fees for trading municipal securities), to also include the regulation of municipal advisors (that earn fees for advisory services) and establish rules for their activities.[52]

On March 10, 2014, the SEC's Division of Enforcement created the Municipalities Continuing Disclosure Cooperation Initiative (MCDC).[53] The MCDC provides issuers and underwriters the opportunity to self-report any material misstatements in bond offering documents (within the last five years of any primary offerings) as well as to comply with continuing disclosures as required by SEC Rule 15c2-12.[54] The objective of MCDC is to encourage issuers to voluntarily correct misrepresentations rather than wait for them to be detected, thereby increasing transparency in the municipal bond markets. The deadline for self-reporting was September 10, 2014, for underwriters (broker-dealers) and December 1, 2014, for issuers.[55]

In addition, the GASB has announced Statement 67 and Statement 68 to further define the requirements for the reporting of accounting and financial information related to municipal pension funding.

- Statement 67, Financial Reporting for Pension Plans, pertains to disclosures primarily for pension beneficiaries and other stakeholders. Examples of information likely to be of concern to beneficiaries include items such as total (employee and employer) pension contributions, predicted rates of returns, and overall performance trends. Statement 67 amends existing Statement 25 to require greater disclosures about material ("decision-usefulness") pension fund details in the notes that accompany the financial statements as well as in the required supplementary information. Statement 67 went into effect for fiscal years beginning after June 15, 2013.[56]
- Statement 68, Accounting and Financial Reporting for Pensions, pertains to disclosures primarily for taxpayers and creditors.[57] Statement 68 amends existing Statement 27 to require that the reporting of pension liabilities occur in the official, accrual based financial statements (rather than mentioned as supplementary information). Statement 68 went into effect for fiscal years beginning after June 15, 2014. This requirement is likely to result in the reporting of larger expenses and liabilities for states and municipalities, arguably providing more complete financial representations.[58]

Although greater transparency and more complete disclosures arguably may be more beneficial for investors, investor reactions are difficult to predict. Some municipal investors may be comfortable with the level and types of financial risks held in their portfolios as long as they are made fully aware; others may be less comfortable. Better disclosures may attract some investors but deter others because risk appetites and tolerance levels are diverse, thus making it difficult to predict how credit flows to municipalities would change with greater transparency. Likewise, it is ambiguous whether improved disclosures would decrease or increase the need for possible federal government intervention, perhaps in the form of financial guarantees. Greater transparency theoretically would be expected to reduce bondholder speculation and, therefore, the possibility of a financial panic. In contrast, greater transparency might reduce the demand for municipal securities, and federal government interventions might still be necessary to reassure investors and support the flow of credit to public-sector entities.

Congressional Efforts to Improve Transparency

The Public Employee Pension Transparency Act (H.R. 1628) and its companion bill of the same name (S. 779) were introduced in the 113th Congress. These bills proposed to foster greater disclosure by encouraging use of reporting requirements specified in the bills for state or local government employee pension benefit plans. The bills would have also removed the federal tax exemption on municipal bond yields during any period in which the issuing locality failed to comply with reporting requirements. In addition, the bills would have exempted the United States from any liabilities associated with shortfalls in any state or local government employee pension plan. These bills may have resulted in increased transparency, but it is unclear whether they would have increased or decreased investor participation in the municipal bond market.

Incentives for Depository Bank Holdings of Municipal Bonds

When deciding whether to hold municipal bonds, all investors, including financial institutions typically consider their rates of return (or yields) as well as the various types of risk factors previously discussed. In addition, the total profitability for institutional investors would be affected by the funding costs (i.e., the cost to borrow the funds necessary to purchase municipals), the tax treatment, and the safety and soundness costs to hold municipal securities (as reflected in related capital requirements). Some of the legislative and regulatory factors that influence banks to hold municipal bonds are listed below.

- Congress passed the Community Reinvestment Act (CRA) of 1977 to encourage federally insured banking institutions to make sufficient credit available in the local areas in which they were chartered and acquiring deposits.[59] Banks have a wide variety of options to serve the credit needs in the geographical area where they acquire deposits.[60] During CRA examinations, banks may receive CRA consideration for holding municipal bonds that promote economic development in their assigned local areas.
- Although the interest from municipal bond investments is not subject to federal tax when held by individuals, the interest is subject to federal taxes when held by banks. The Tax Equity and Fiscal Responsibility Act of 1982[61] limited the interest deduction on municipals for banks to 85%; the Deficit Reduction Act of 1984[62] further reduced the deduction to 80%. The Tax Reform Act of 1986 eliminated the interest deduction on municipals for banks, but exemptions were made for "qualified tax-exempt obligations" up to a $10 million annual limit.[63] Specifically, banks must pay taxes on the interest income earned from municipals, but they may deduct 80% of the costs incurred to fund municipals that satisfy certain regulatory requirements.
- Under Basel III capital requirements for banks, the dollar amount of municipal bond holdings are multiplied by an assigned *risk weight* that is subsequently used in the calculation of the required capital reserves a bank must maintain. The current risk weight assigned to a general obligation bond backed by the full faith and credit of the public-sector entity is 20%; the risk weight is 50% for issuances that are expected to be repaid with revenues from a project rather than general tax funds.[64] Should the status of a particular set of municipal securities change to nonperforming, the risk weight applied to the outstanding balance for troubled bank loans increases to 150%, resulting in greater capitalization pressures. For example, suppose a banking institution is holding a set of municipal bond obligations that

experience a ratings downgrade such that the securities are no longer investment grade.[65] Because the secondary municipal bond market is not liquid, disposal of these riskier assets is unlikely to occur quickly especially if the market value of these securities decline. Banking institutions would need to increase their regulatory capital against the value of the downgraded assets until they have been sold or written off the balance sheet as losses.

Congress has shown willingness to foster greater credit access for public infrastructure spending for possible economic stimulus. For example,

- The American Recovery and Reinvestment Act of 2009 (P.L. 111-5) included provisions allowing for the temporary issuance (before January 1, 2011) of a tax-credit bond, the Build America Bond (BAB), which paid bondholders (including banks) a federal tax credit equal to 35% of taxable interest. This development coincides with the observed rise in the share of bank municipal holdings in 2009 (as shown in Figure 1), because the after-tax interest income earned from BABs would increase for banks relative to traditional municipal bonds.
- The Move America Act of 2015 (S. 1186) proposes to “expand tax-exempt private activity bonds and create a new infrastructure tax credit,” which allows states to pursue infrastructure projects, was introduced in the Senate.[66]
- The Municipal Bond Market Support Act of 2015 (H.R. 2229) was introduced on May 1, 2015. H.R. 2229 would increase the annual municipal debt limit that could be exempt from $10 million to $30 million on the amount of tax-exempt obligations a small issuer may issue for a bank to purchase.[67] The bill also would allow for a higher increase in the annual inflation adjustment. Banks would be able to increase their investment in tax-exempt municipal securities up to the higher limits. The reduction in federal tax liabilities would increase the expected rate of return of municipal bond investments for banks, possibly increasing their incentive to hold more bonds.

Liquidity Requirements for Depositories

In September 2008, the short-term overnight funds market collapsed when financial institutions suddenly refused to make short-term loans to other financial institutions after reports of other distressed financial institutions, an example of a systemic risk event.[68] The panic response by numerous financial institutions to discontinue their participation in financial markets arguably prompted the Federal Reserve to intervene and provide liquidity to the financial system.[69] The Federal Reserve and other federal banking agencies proposed strengthening liquidity regulations, calling for depository banking institutions with $10 billion or more in assets to hold more *high quality liquid assets* (HQLA) in their portfolios.[70] In the final rule, the qualifying liquid assets have been defined over various ranges (i.e., level 1, level 2A, and level 2B), with level 1 being the most liquid, followed by level 2A and then level 2B being least liquid.[71] The federal banking regulators did not include municipal bonds in any of the HQLA definitions because they observed a wide range of liquidity characteristics for municipal bonds, making it difficult for this class of securities to collectively meet the liquid and readily marketable requirements.

On April 16, 2014, several Members of Congress requested that the Federal Reserve include municipals as part of HQLA.[72] The exclusion of municipal bonds from HQLA eligibility may discourage banks from increasing their municipal holdings, possibly increasing the funding costs for state and local governments. On May 4, 2015, H.R. 2209was introduced "to require the appropriate federal banking agencies to treat certain municipal obligations as level 2A liquid assets, and for other purposes." Because some municipal bonds may trade in relatively more liquid markets compared with others, this bill would allow for a specific subset of municipal bonds satisfying a criteria for liquid and readily-marketable securities to be included in the level 2A HQLA asset definition. The Federal Reserve has issued a proposed rule to allow some municipal bonds with acceptable liquidity characteristics to satisfy one of the HQLA definitions; however, other banking regulators still view municipal bonds to be illiquid for the intrinsic purposes of the rule.[73] If the other federal regulators choose not to adopt rules similar to the Federal Reserve's rule, then holdings of municipals by bank depositories or depository subsidiaries would not apply toward their HQLA requirement even if it can be applied at the bank holding company level.

The Dodd-Frank Wall Street Reform and Consumer Protection Act

The Dodd-Frank Act contained provisions that arguably may influence bank purchases of municipals. One provision is related to the use of credit ratings.[74] The Dodd-Frank Act removed the use of credit ratings from regulatory guidance, and banks now face new guidelines for determining investment grade securities that can be held in their portfolios.[75] An investment grade security is defined as one in which "the issuer of the security has an adequate capacity to meet financial commitments under the security for the projected life of the asset or exposure."[76] Banks must perform credit risk due diligence for the municipal securities they hold, showing that issuers meet the definition of investment grade. Banks may continue to use credit agency ratings in their assessments, but only as a factor among a variety of factors (such as various market comparisons and economic data trends, similar in nature to some of the credit spreads discussed previously) that should be considered. Hence, the costs to hold some municipals, particularly smaller issuances by smaller localities for unique projects, may have risen in cases where regulated institutions must perform additional due diligence to authenticate the risk levels.[77] Furthermore, tens of thousands of municipal bonds are nonrated to reduce borrowing costs, meaning that it may become more challenging for banks to determine whether the bonds are investment grade.[78] As a result, the demand for the highest credit quality municipal bonds may increase whereas the demand to hold bonds by more financially vulnerable issuers may fall.

One provision that arguably may have less influence on bank purchases of municipals is the Volcker Rule. The Volcker Rule prohibits banking entities from proprietary trading activities or the buying and selling of one or more financial instruments for short-term resale (less than 60 days) to benefit from short-term price movements or to realize short-term arbitrage profits. Trading on behalf of customers is permitted so long as the banking entity does not retain beneficial ownership of the instrument.[79]

In a comment letter to the federal banking regulators, the MSRB reported that approximately three-fourths of the firms underwriting and trading municipal securities in FY2011 were covered by a proposed version of the Volcker Rule.[80] The federal bank regulators amended the initial proposal, which exempted municipal bonds from the final rule.[81] The final rule that implements the Volcker Rule still permits banks to engage in the proprietary trading of U.S. government, agency, state, and municipal security obligations.[82] Hence, it is unlikely that any future declines in municipal bond purchases by banks would be attributed to the Volcker Rule.

APPENDIX. THE FINANCIAL HEALTH OF MUNICIPAL BOND ISSUERS

The fiscal status of issuers is essential to understanding the overall health of the municipal bond market. This section presents aggregate statistics about revenues, expenditures, and outstanding debts of state and local governments (before and after the 2007-2009 recession) that may issue municipals to fund expenditures.[83] Although state and local governments do not issue all municipal bonds, the data collected by the U.S. Census Bureau Governments Division are used in this report for brevity. The composite statistics should not be interpreted to mean that an aggregate fiscal health diagnosis would apply equally to all municipal bond issuers. A state could be experiencing a budget crisis while local governments within the same state may be financially sound. Conversely, a state may maintain a better financial situation than some of its localities. The tax (revenue-generating) policies and expenditure patterns also vary for all state and local public-sector entities. Hence, the aggregate data would not capture the financial health of each locality, but the trends may help identify the broad challenges faced by municipal bond market issuers.

Public-sector entities generally have *current (annual) operating budgets* that are determined by current revenues and expenses. Current revenues are generated by items such as taxes, fees, user charges, and intergovernmental aid. Current expenses include items such as employee salaries, payment for services, and interest payments on debt. For the most part, state and local governments are required to balance their current operating budgets. Short-term liabilities that are incurred and repaid within a year would not show up in the year-end financial statements.[84] Longterm obligations expected to be repaid over a period greater than one year and funded by municipal bonds would typically appear in the *capital budget*. The payment of annual interest on long-term liabilities, however, should appear in the operating budget. For example, suppose a public-sector entity has a long-term financial obligation to pay for an infrastructure project. Annual interest payments to creditors such as municipal bond holders would be accounted for in the current operating budget; the total obligation would appear in the long-term capital budget.

Using U.S. Census Bureau's data, *Figure A-1* shows the aggregate trends in state and local governments' current revenues collected from their *own sources* (e.g., taxes, general revenues), current revenues that include federal government appropriations, and current expenditures. All years are measured by fiscal years (between July 1 and June 30) rather than calendar years. For the most part, current state and local government revenues have been able to meet current expenditures with the help of federal government funding. From FY2000 to FY2007, current revenues from own sources tracked current expenditures rather closely. The gap between current revenues from own sources and current expenditures was narrowing. After FY2007, however, the trend in aggregate current revenue fell below the trend in current expenditures. The trend in current revenues stopped declining by FY2009, but the gap between current revenues and current expenditures has since widened significantly.

In early 2014, credit rating agencies downgraded the credit quality of an estimated 20% of state and local governments.[85] Downgrades typically translate into higher borrowing costs for state and local municipalities to finance their expenditures. Closing the gaps may ultimately require state and local governments to either raise taxes, reduce spending, or both. In the meantime, state and local public-sector entities appear to have the ability to cover their operating expenses (in absence of periods of recession) after factoring in revenues from the federal government.

Capital budgets are typically used to finance long-term investments, such as infrastructure, education, among other things. Municipal bonds are typically issued to finance long-term investment expenditures that would be expected to appear in the capital budgets. *Figure A-1* shows the outstanding balance of aggregate debts that will be repaid over periods lasting longer than one year. From 2000 to 2012, the outstanding debt levels of U.S. state and local governments doubled from $1.45 trillion to $2.94 trillion. The rise in aggregate revenues, however, has not kept pace with the rise in outstanding aggregate debts. Aggregate own-source revenues for the states and local governments over the 2000-2012 period increased from $1.65 trillion to $1.97 trillion, representing a 22.0% increase. When federal transfers are included in aggregate revenues, the increase from $1.94 trillion to $3.03 trillion represents an increase of approximately 56.2%. Hence, the aggregate debt outstanding of state and local governments grew at a faster pace over the last decade than aggregate revenues. Rising capital budget obligations may translate into greater debt outstanding and, therefore, greater financial risk for municipal bond investors.

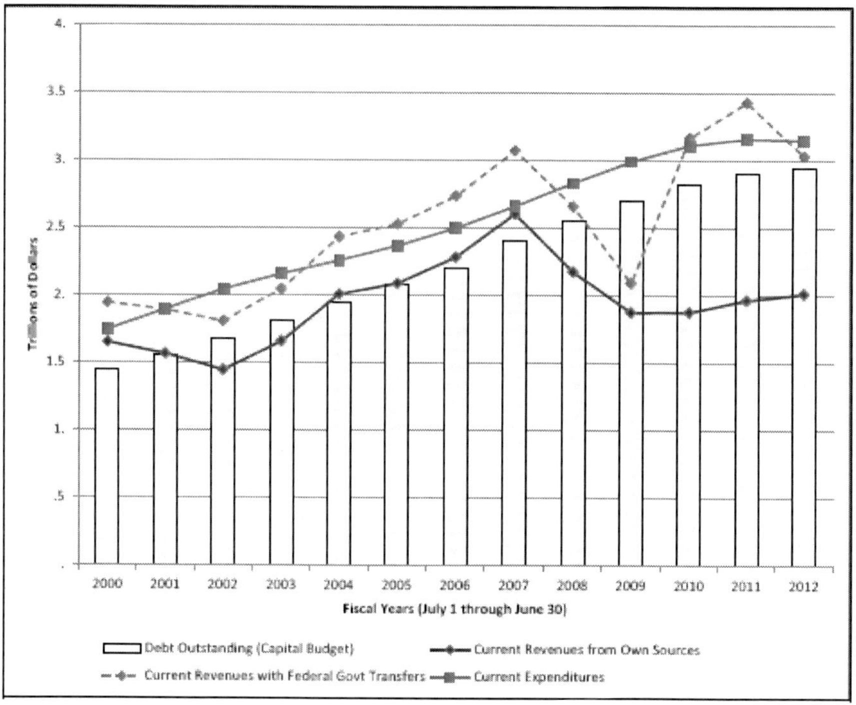

Source: The Congressional Research Service using data from the U.S. Census Bureau Governments Division.

Figure A-1. State and Local Government Finances Summary: Total Revenues, Expenditures, and Debt Outstanding. (FY2000-FY2012)

Another important source of rising state and local obligations may arguably be unfunded pension liabilities.[86] Reliable estimates, however, are difficult to obtain because certain public-sector entities choose not to disclose these liabilities in their capital budgets.[87] The Census Bureau reports that total annual contributions into state and local pension systems are currently trending below total annual payments made to beneficiaries, as shown in *Figure A-2*.[88] Furthermore, the earnings on pension fund investments are extremely volatile, making it difficult to rely on them to cover annual shortfalls consistently. The assets in local pension funds consist primarily of nongovernmental securities (e.g., corporate stocks and bonds, foreign and international securities, mortgages, and other high-risk investments). Municipal pensions also invest in real estate, which is found in the *total other investments* category. Less risky investments (e.g., U.S. federal government securities, cash, and shorter-term liquid assets) comprise a significantly smaller share of the pension fund portfolio. The higher financial risk associated with the longer-term investments explain the fluctuations of investment earnings.[89]

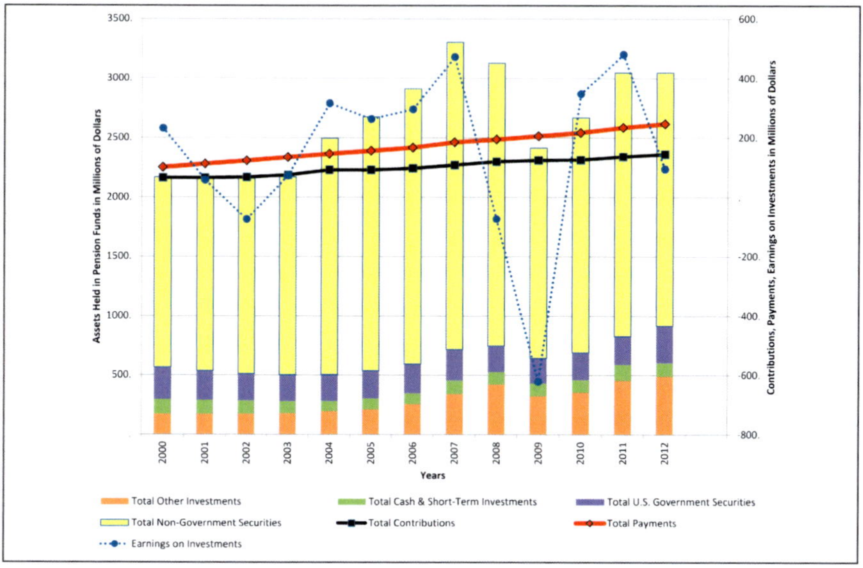

Source: U.S. Census Bureau Governments Division.
Note: CRS Computations.

Figure A-2. Aggregate State Pension Fund Annual Contributions, Payments, and Portfolio Holdings.

Tax-advantaged qualified tuition programs, also known as 529 college savings plans, may be considered another source of rising indebtedness for some states.[90] The 529 plans allow for a contributor (e.g., a parent) to establish a savings account for a beneficiary (e.g., the child) in which withdrawals are not subject to federal, state, and local taxes as long as the distributions are used to pay for qualified higher education expenses.[91] Tuition for a specified number of academic semesters, attendance to designated public institutions within the locality, and other requirements are examples of qualified higher education expenses eligible for the tax benefit. In addition, some 529 plans function as prepaid tuition plans, allowing contributors to pay future education expenses at current or present day prices.[92] States or local governments provide their full faith and credit guarantee for the 529 plans they sponsor.[93] The state or local municipality bears the tuition inflation risk if the earnings on the invested contributions do not fully cover the future (higher) education costs. In response to concerns about rising education costs, some states have closed their 529 tuition plans to new participants, put plans on hold, and suspended operations.[94]

End Notes

[1] See Municipal Securities Rulemaking Board (MSRB), "How the Market Works," at http://www.msrb.org/MunicipalBond-Market/How-the-Market-Works.aspx.

[2] The estimated 1.5 million municipal bonds is 20 times the number of corporate bonds. See Commissioner Luis A. Aguilar, Statement on Making the Municipal Securities Market More Transparent, Liquid, and Fair, U.S. Securities and Exchange Commission, February 13, 2015, at http://www.sec.gov/news/statement/making-municipal-securitiesmarket-more-transparent-liquid-fair.html.

[3] Not all state and local bond issues are exempt from federal taxes. For example, returns from pension obligation bonds, issued by state and local governments to fund employee pension retirement funds, are taxable at the federal level.

[4] P.L. 94-29, 89 Stat. 97.

[5] See U.S. Government Accountability Office (GAO), Securities and Exchange Commission: Opportunities Exist to Improve Oversight of Self-Regulatory Organizations, GAO-08-33, November 2007, at http://www.gao.gov/new.items/d0833.pdf.

[6] See MSRB Registration, at http://www.msrb.org/Rules-and-Interpretations/MSRB-Registration.aspx.

[7] The distressed financial situation of the Commonwealth of Puerto Rico, which is not the primary focus of this report, serves as an example of financial distress attributed to a widening fiscal gap.

[8] Despite differences in legal status, the terms bond and loan will be used interchangeably throughout this report; the terms issuer and borrower will be used interchangeably; and the terms bondholder or investor will be used interchangeably with lender.

[9] See CRS Report R43345, Shadow Banking: Background and Policy Issues, by Edward V. Murphy; and CRS In Focus IF10202, Collateralized Loan Obligations (CLOs), Structure, Use, and Implementation of the Volcker Rule, by Edward V. Murphy.

[10] Board of Governors of the Federal Reserve System, Financial Accounts of the United States (Flow of Funds, Balance Sheets, and Integrated Macroeconomic Accounts, Historical Annual Tables 2005-2014), Table L.211, at http://www.federalreserve.gov/releases/z1/Current/annuals/a2005-2014.pdf.

[11] See Lisa Lambert, "Households Pull Back More from U.S. Municipal Market: Fed," Reuters, June 5, 2014, at http://www.reuters.com/article/2014/06/05/us-usa-municipals-idUSKBNOEG27Q20140605; and Robert Slavin, "Data Show Changes in Muni Buying Patterns," The Bond Buyer, May 1, 2012, at http://www.bondbuyer.com/issues/121_84/ hol ders-municipal-debt-1039214-1.html.

[12] See Gary S. Corner, Emily Dai, and Daigo Gubo, Could Rising Municipal Securities Holdings Increase Community Banks' Risk Profiles?, Federal Reserve Bank of St. Louis, Central Banker, fall 2013, at https://www.stlouisfed.org/publications/ cb/articles/?id=2447.

[13] Money market deposit accounts are similar to interest-bearing checking accounts offered by federally insured depository institutions for their depositors that typically may keep relatively large deposit balances. By contrast, funds deposited in money market mutual accounts offered by investment banks are not federally insured. Mutual fund accounts may

serve as short-term parking vehicles for investors moving funds between longer-term investments (facilitated by the same investment bank). These accounts, unlike insured money market depository accounts, pay a slightly higher interest rate. Hence, investors wishing to invest in pools of municipal securities may be willing to obtain a higher return by forgoing the added safety net of federal deposit insurance, particularly if they do not perceive higher than usual repayment risks in the municipal bond market. For more information on federal depository insurance and institutions, see CRS Report R41718, Federal Deposit Insurance for Banks and Credit Unions, by Darryl E. Getter.

[14] See Carla Fried, "Municipal Bonds, Stung Again," The New York Times, October 5, 2013, at http://www.nytimes.com/2013/10/06/business/mutfund/municipal-bonds-stung-again.html.

[15] U.S. Securities and Exchange Commission (SEC), Report on the Municipal Securities Market, July 31, 2012, at http://www.sec.gov/news/studies/2012/munireport073112.pdf.Municis.

[16] See Jose A. Lopez, What is Liquidity Risk?, Federal Reserve Bank of San Francisco, FRBSF Economic Letter, October 24, 2008, at http://www.frbsf.org/economic-research/publications/economic-letter/2008/october/liquidity-risk/.

[17] Ibid, p. 21.

[18] See Commissioner Luis A. Aguilar, Statement on Making the Municipal Securities Market More Transparent, Liquid, and Fair, U.S. Securities and Exchange Commission, February 13, 2015, at http://www.sec.gov/news/statement/making-municipal-securities-market-more-transparent-liquid-fair.html.

[19] See U.S. Securities and Exchange Commission, Report on the Municipal Securities Market, July 31, 2012, at http://www.sec.gov/news/studies/2012/munireport073112.pdf.Municis.

[20] See U.S. Government Accountability Office (GAO), Municipal Securities: Overview of Market Structure, Pricing, and Regulation, GAO-12-265, January 2012, at http://www.gao.gov/assets/590/587714.pdf; and Burton Hollifield, SEC Municipal Bond Panel, Presentation, Washington, DC, April 2013, at https://www.sec.gov/spotlight/fixed-income-markets/fixed-income-markets-municipal-bonds-hollifield.pdf.

[21] See Electronic Municipal Market Access (EMMA) website at http://www.emma.msrb.org/.

[22] See Jason Appleson, Eric Parsons, and Andrew Haughwout, "The Untold Story of Municipal Bond Defaults," Liberty Street Economics, August 15, 2012, at http://libertystreeteconomics.newyorkfed.org/2012/08/the-untold-storyof-municipal-bond-defaults.html.

[23] See S&P Dow Jones Indices, McGraw Hill Financial, Energy-Related Municipal Bonds Help Push the S&P Municipal Bond Index Default Rate to a 3-Year High in 2014, Fixed Income Update, New York, NY, January 2015, at http://www.spindices.com/documents/research/fixed-income-updates-muni-bond-default-rate-dec-2014.pdf; and Robert Slavin, "Defaults Reached Record in 2014," The Bond Buyer, January 13, 2015, at http://www.bondbuyer.com/news/ markets-buy-side/defaults-reached-record-in-2014-1069491-1.html; and Liz Farmer, "S&P Defends Higher Municipal Credit Ratings," GOVERNING, October 9, 2014, at http://www.governing.com/news/headlines/gov-credit-ratingupgrade-increase-reasons.html.

[24] For example, see National Association of State Budget Officers, "2014 Fact: State and Municipal Bankruptcy, Municipal Bonds, State and Local Pensions," Winter 2014, at http://www.nasbo.org/sites/default/files/pdf/BankruptcyBonds-Pensions%20Fact% 20Sheet.pdf.

[25] A rated bond is one that has received from an independent bond rating agency a grade based upon the issuer's financial strength and ability to repay the principal and interest in a timely manner. A database consisting of both rated and unrated municipal bonds shows that 2,521 municipals defaulted over the 1970-2011 period, compared with 71 defaults reported by a

private ratings agency. See Jason Appleson, Eric Parsons, and Andrew Haughwout, The Untold Story of Municipal Bond Defaults, Federal Reserve Bank of New York, Liberty Street Economics, August 15, 2012, at http://libertystreeteconomics.newyorkfed.org/2012/08/the-untold-story-of-municipal-bond-defaults.html.

[26] See the Appendix.

[27] For example, see Brian Chappatta and Tim Jones, "Chicago Cut to 3 Levels Above Junk by Moody's on Pensions," Bloomberg, March 5, 2014, at http://www.bloomberg.com/news/2014-03-05/chicago-cut-to-3-levels-above-junk-bymoody-s-on-pensions.html.

[28] See Christine Albano, "Puerto Rico and Detroit: Investors Tread Fine Line Between Value and Concern," The Bond Buyer, September 23, 2013, at http://www.bondbuyer.com/issues/122_184/puerto-rico-and-detroit-investors-treadbetween-value-and-concern-1055832-1.html.

[29] Some municipalities that have filed bankruptcy include Gould, AK (April 2008); Vallejo, CA (May 2008); Westfall Township, PA (April 2009); Washington Park, IL (July 2009); Central Falls, RI (August 1, 2011); Boise County, ID (September 8, 2011); Harrisburg, PA (October 2011); Jefferson County, AL (November 9, 2011); Stockton, CA (June 28, 2012); Mammoth Lakes, CA (July 3, 2012); San Bernardino, CA (August 1, 2012); and Detroit, MI (July 18, 2013). See "Which American Municipalities Have Filed for Bankruptcy?" PBS NEWSHOUR, February 8, 2014, at http://www.pbs.org/newshour/updates/municipalities-declared-bankruptcy/; Micheline Maynard, "Detroit Is Eligible For Bankruptcy, And City Pensions Are At Risk," Forbes, December 3, 2013, at http://www.forbes.com/sites/michelinemaynard/2013/12/03/detroit-is-eligible-for-bankruptcy-and-city-pensions-are-at-risk/.

[30] Bond insurance guarantees bond purchasers (i.e., investors) that interest payments will be made on time and principal will eventually be returned if the issuers default. Municipalities facing financial difficulties, therefore, may still receive high credit ratings for their bond issuances if they purchase bond insurance from a highly rated monoline insurance company. Monoline insurers are not allowed to provide life, automobile, or property insurance; they may only provide guarantees for financial obligations. The insurance may be provided either in the form of a traditional insurance policy, which would be subject to state insurance regulation, or in the form of a credit default swap, which is a financial contract not subject to capitalization requirements that may be traded on the open market. See CRS Report RL34364, Bond Insurers: Issues for the 110th Congress, by Baird Webel and Darryl E. Getter.

[31] See Wells Fargo, "Deterioration of Monoline Insurance Companies and the Repercussions for Municipal Bonds," Wells Fargo Advantage Funds, November 2008, at https://www.wellsfargoadvantagefunds.com/pdf/whitepapers/monoline_insurance_muni_ bonds.pdf.

[32] See Oliver Renick and Maria Bonnello, "Bond Insurance Then & Now: The Revival of an Industry," The Bond Buyer, April 30, 2014, at http://www.bondbuyer.com/issues/123_83/bond-insurance-then-and-now-revival-of-industry1062071-1.html.

[33] During the 1800s, episodes of economic contraction, including the Panic of 1873, were characterized by municipal bondholder panics. See Mayraj Fahim, Municipal Bonds Have Been Issued by U.S. Local Governments Since 1812, City Mayors Foundation, 2012, at http://www.citymayors.com/finance/bonds.html#Anchor-47383.

[34] An investors' run in the municipal bond market is analogous to a bank run in which depositors suddenly withdraws their funds out of a bank that is believed to be insolvent or unable to repay.

[35] See U.S. Financial Stability Oversight Council, Annual Report, 2015, at http://www.treasury.gov/initiatives/fsoc/ studies-reports/Documents/2015%20FSOC%20Annual%20Report.pdf.

[36] See Mary Williams Walsh, "S&P Lowers Puerto Rico Debt to Junk Status," February 4, 2014, at http://dealbook.nytimes.com/2014/02/04/s-p-lowers-puerto-rico-debt-to-junk-status/ ?_r=0.

[37] 15 U.S.C. §77a et seq.

[38] The federal tax exemption for municipal bonds was originally not intended to provide financial assistance to states; instead, it is rooted in the separation of federal and state governments, specifically the intergovernmental tax immunity doctrine as prescribed by the Tenth Amendment of the U.S. Constitution. See Ronald P. Bernardi, Justin Formas, and Allison White, Tax Exempt Municipal Bonds: The Case for an Efficient, Low-Cost, Job-Creating Tax Expenditure, Bernardi Securities, Inc. Municipal Bond Specialists, December 2011, at http://www.lumesis.com/pdf/BernardiSecurities-Inc-White-Paper.pdf. In the Pollock vs. Farmers Loan Trust (1894) decision, the Supreme Court upheld protection of states from federal interference with their respective borrowing ability; see Joy A. Howard, "Municipal Bond Disclosure—History, Requirements and Services Provided by WMFS," WM Financial Strategies, at http://www.munibondadvisor.com/Disclosure.htm. In Baker v. South Carolina (56 USLW 4311 (April 20, 1988)), however, the Supreme Court "held that there is no constitutional barrier to the imposition of Federal income taxes on interest received by holders of state and local government obligations." For more information, see Bruce F. Davie and Dennis Zimmerman, "Tax-Exempt Bonds After the South Carolina Decision," Tax Notes, June 27, 1988, p. 1573.

[39] 15 U.S.C. §78a et seq.

[40] P.L. 94-29; 15 U.S.C. §78o-4(d).

[41] The SEC has the authority to require publicly listed private-sector companies to follow GAAP accounting standards, established by the Financial Accounting Standards Board (FASB), when preparing their financial statements. See CRS Report R43087, Who Regulates Whom and How? An Overview of U.S. Financial Regulatory Policy for Banking and Securities Markets, by Edward V. Murphy.

[42] See U.S. Securities and Exchange Commission, "SEC Charges State of New Jersey for Fraudulent Municipal Bond Offerings," press release, August 18, 2010, at http://www.sec.gov/news/press/2010/2010-152.htm; and Government Finance Officers' Association of New Jersey, "Standard Setter Amends N.J. Pension Accounting," The Report, vol. 2, issue 1, (winter 2012), at http://c.ymcdn.com/sites/www.gfoanj.org/resource/resmgr/Winter_Newsletter.pdf.

[43] National Association of State Budget Offices (NASBO), "Budget Processes in the States," summer 2008, at https://www.nasbo.org/sites/default/files/BP_2008.pdf; NASBO, "A Note About State Deficits/Shortfalls," at http://www.nasbo.org/about-nasbo/press-room/glossary-terms; E. Matthew Quigley, Amanda Lydon "Dealing with Deficits: How New England States are Managing the Fiscal Crisis," Federal Reserve Bank of Boston, fall 2002, no. 29, at http://www.bostonfed.org/economic/neff/neff29/defecits.pdf; and National Conference of State Legislatures, NCSL Fiscal Brief: State Balanced Budget Provisions, October 2010, at http://www.ncsl.org/documents/fiscal/ statebalancedbudgetprovisions2010.pdf.

[44] See Mary Williams Walsh, "Judge Approves Bankruptcy Exit for Stockton, California," New York Times, October 30, 2014, at http://dealbook.nytimes.com/2014/10/30/judge-approves-bankruptcy-exit-for-stockton-calif/?emc=edit_dlbkpm_20141030&nl=business&nlid=69190179&_r=0.

[45] See Annette Thau, Notes on the Current State of the Muni Bond Market, American Association of Individual Investors, May 2012, at http://www.aaii.com/journal/article/notes-on-the-current-state-of-the-muni-bond-market.touch.

[46] See Bond Dealers of America, "Advocacy—Priorities in 2014," at http://www. bdamerica. org/advocacy.

[47] See U.S. Securities and Exchange Commission, Commissioner Elisse B. Walter, "Key Note Address at the National Association of Bond Lawyers (NALB) 35th Bond Attorney's Workshop," San Antonio, TX, October 28, 2010, at http://www.sec.gov/news/ speech/2010/spch102810ebw.htm.

[48] See CRS Legal Sidebar, SEC Charges States with Fraud for Understating Municipal Bond Exposure, by Michael V. Seitzinger. A list of SEC charges and sanctions against states and municipalities for improper disclosures of risk to investors may be found on the SEC's "Office of Municipal Securities" website under "Cases & Materials," at http://www. sec.gov/municipal.

[49] 17 C.F.R. §240. There are certain exemptions from Rule 15c2-12. See Municipal Securities Rulemaking Board, "SEC Rule 15c2-12: Continuing Disclosures," at http://www.msrb. org/msrb1/pdfs/SECRule15c2-12.pdf.

[50] See Commissioner Luis A. Aguilar, Statement on Making the Municipal Securities Market More Transparent, Liquid, and Fair, U.S. Securities and Exchange Commission, February 13, 2015, at http://www.sec.gov/news/statement/making-municipal-securities-market-more-transparent-liquid-fair.html.

[51] P.L. 111-203.

[52] For an overview of these regulatory changes, see U.S. Congress, Senate Committee on Banking, Housing, and Urban Affairs, Testimony on Enhanced Investor Protection After the Financial Crisis—MSRB's Implementation of the Dodd-Frank Wall Street Reform and Consumer Protection Act and Investor Protection, Enhanced Investor Protection After the Financial Crisis, 112th Cong., 1st sess., July 12, 2011, at http://www.msrb.org/msrb1/pdfs/ TestimonyonImplementationofDodd-FrankandInvestorProtection.pdf.

[53] See U.S. Securities and Exchange Commission, "SEC Launches Enforcement Cooperation Initiative for Municipal Issuers and Underwriters," press release, March 10, 2014, at http://www.sec.gov/News/PressRelease/Detail/ PressRelease/1370541090828.

[54] See U.S. Securities and Exchange Commission, "SEC: Municipalities Continuing Disclosure Cooperating Initiative," at http://www.sec.gov/divisions/enforce/municipalities-continuing-disclosure-cooperation-initiative.shtml.

[55] The SEC has standardized possible settlement terms for various violations, but no assurances are offered with respect to individual liabilities. As reported by the SEC, the issuers will not face any monetary penalties and underwriters will face monetary penalties based on the amount of the offering. For those that do not self-report but are found to be in violation of the Rule, SEC gives no guarantees as to the terms of the settlement.

[56] GASB, Summary of Statement No. 67 Financial Reporting for Pension Plans—An Amendment of GASB Statement No. 25, Norwalk, CT, http://www.gasb.org/cs/Content Server?site=GASB&c=Pronouncement_C&pagename=GASB%2FPronouncement_C%2F GASBSummaryPage&cid=1176160219444.

[57] GASB, Summary of Statement No. 68 Accounting Financial Reporting for Pensions—An Amendment of GASB Statement No. 27, Norwalk, CT, http://www.gasb.org/cs/ ContentServer?site=GASB&c=Pronouncement_C&pagename=GASB%2FPronoun cement _C%2FGASBSummaryPage&cid=1176160219492.

[58] GASB Statement 71 amends paragraph 137 of Statement 68 to add further clarification on transition issues from Statement 27 to Statement 68. GASB, Summary of Statement No. 71 - Pension Transition for Contributions Made Subsequent to the Measurement Pension Transition for Contributions Made Subsequent to the Measurement, Norwalk, CT, November 2013, http://www.gasb.org/cs/ContentServer?c=Pronouncement_C&pagename=GASB%2FPronouncement_C%2FGASBSummaryPage&cid=1176163785801.

[59] P.L. 95-128, 12 U.S.C. §2901-2908. For more information, see CRS Report R43661, The Effectiveness of the Community Reinvestment Act, by Darryl E. Getter.

[60] Rather than impose lending quotas, banks receive Community Reinvestment Act (CRA) ratings. A favorable CRA rating may allow a bank to get permission from its primary regulator to engage in prospective profit opportunity, such as a future merger.

[61] P.L. 97-248.

[62] P.L. 98-369.

[63] P.L. 99-514. For more information, see Peter Fortune, "The Municipal Bank Market, Part I: Politics, Taxes, and Yields," Federal Reserve Bank of Boston, New England Economic Review, September/October 1991, at http://www.bostonfed.org/economic/neer/neer1991/neer591b.pdf; and Howard P. Estes, Jr., Municipal Bonds: Good News for Community Banks, Spotts Fain, February 13, 2014, at http://www.spottsfain.com/publications/295-municipalbonds-good-news-community-banks.

[64] For a discussion of bank asset risk weighting and an example, see CRS Report R42744, U.S. Implementation of the Basel Capital Regulatory Framework, by Darryl E. Getter.

[65] For example, see Darrell Preston, Elizabeth Campbell, and Brian Chappatta, "Chicago Faces $2.2 Billion Bank Payout After Rating Cut to Junk," May 13, 2015, at http://www.bloomberg.com/news/articles/2015-05-13/chicagofaces-2-2-billion-bank-payout-after-rating-cut-to-junk.

[66] See The United States Senate Committee on Finance, "Wyden and Hoeven Introduce Move America Program to Boost Infrastructure Investment," press release, May 4, 2015, at http://www.finance.senate.gov/newsroom/ranking/ release/?id=27efdfd3-33b3-4524-9cde-0ef0bc875a95.

[67] See Letter from American Hospital Association, Bond Dealers of America, and Independent Community Bankers of America et al. to Honorables Tom Reed, John Larson, Richard Neal, Randy Hultgren, Members of the U.S. House of Representatives, September 19, 2014, http://www.icba.org/files/ICBASites/PDFs/ltr091914.pdf.

[68] Systemic risk often refers to a sudden loss of confidence (or panic) by financial market participants following a liquidity disruption, a default, a decline in asset prices, or even an expected decline in asset prices. Systemic risk runs are often discussed in the context of banking panics, when depositors suddenly attempt to withdraw their deposits from banks before they fail or become insolvent. A systemic risk run, however, may occur in any financial market. Systemic risk would also be analogous to a heightened level of headline risk, discussed in U.S. Government Accountability Office, Municipal Securities: Overview of Market Structure, Pricing, and Regulation, GAO-12-265, January 2012, at http://www.gao.gov/assets/590/587714.pdf.

[69] See CRS Report RL34427, Financial Turmoil: Federal Reserve Policy Responses, by Marc Labonte.

[70] See Board of Governors of the Federal Reserve System, "Federal Reserve Board proposes rule to strengthen liquidity positions of large financial institutions," press release, October 24, 2013, at http://www.federalreserve.gov/newsevents/ press/bcreg/20131024a.htm; CRS Report R42744, U.S. Implementation of the Basel Capital Regulatory Framework, by

Darryl E. Getter; and CRS In Focus, The Liquidity Coverage Ratio (LCR), by Marc Labonte.

[71] See U.S. Department of Treasury, OCC, the Federal Reserve System, and the FDIC, "Liquidity Coverage Ratio: Liquidity Risk Measurement Standards," 79 Federal Register 197, October 10, 2014, pp. 61440-61541, at http://www.gpo.gov/fdsys/pkg/FR-2014-10-10/pdf/2014-22520.pdf.

[72] Fifteen Members of Congress from the New York congressional delegation sent the comment letter. See Comment Letter to the Board of Governors of the Federal Reserve System, at http://www.federalreserve.gov/SECRS/2014/May/20140515/R-1466/R-1466_050614_129464_560420342526_1.pdf.

[73] See Board of Governors of the Federal Reserve System, "Regulation WW: Liquidity Coverage Ratio: Treatment of U.S. Municipal Securities as High-Quality Liquid Assets," press release, May 21, 2015, at http://www.federalreserve.gov/newsevents/press/bcreg/20150521a.htm; and Andrew Ackerman and Victoria McGrane, "Fed Is Expected to Shift on Muni Bonds," The Wall Street Journal, April 15, 2015, at http://www.wsj.com/articles/fed-is-expected-to-shift-on-muni-bonds-1429232200.

[74] See EMMA, "Understanding Credit Ratings," at http://emma.msrb.org/Emma He lp/UnderstandingCreditRatings.aspx. Credit ratings may also be used to help determine municipal bond prices. A strong credit rating allows issuers to pay lower yields to investors. Investors holding lower- and non-rated bonds (that generally trade even less frequently than higher-rated municipals) expect to be compensated higher rates of return.

[75] § 939A. See U.S. Department of the Treasury, Office of the Comptroller of the Currency (OCC), "Alternatives to the Use of External Credit Ratings in the Regulations of the OCC," OCC Bulletin 2012-18, June 26, 2012, at http://www.occ.gov/news-issuances/bulletins/2012/bulletin-2012-18.html; Christopher McBride, "Investing in Securities Without Relying on External Credit Ratings," Community Banking Connections, Federal Reserve System, Second Quarter 2013, at http://www.communitybankingconnections.org/articles/ 2013/Q2/Investing-in-SecuritiesWithout-Relying-on-External-Credit-Ratings.cfm; and Federal Deposit Insurance Corporation (FDIC), Investment Securities—New Rules for Assessing Credit Risk, 2014 FDIC Chicago Region Regulatory Conference Call Series, https://www.fdic.gov/news/conferences/chicago_region/2014-04-24.pdf.

[76] See U.S. Department of the Treasury, OCC, "Alternatives to the Use of External Credit Ratings in the Regulations of the OCC," 77 Federal Register 35253-35259, June 13, 2012.

[77] The SEC also issued a rule that arguably could narrow the array of securities that money market funds would be permitted to purchase. See "Removal of Certain References to Credit Ratings and Amendment to the Issuer Diversification Requirement in the Money Market Fund Rule," at http://www.sec.gov/rules/proposed/2014/ic31184.pdf; and Kyle Glazer, "SEC Proposal to Remove Rating References from MMF Rule Sparks Concerns," Bond Buyer, October 21, 2014, at http://www.bondbuyer.com/news/washington-securities-law/sec-proposal-to-remove-rating-references-from-mmf-rule-sparks-concerns-1067207-1.html?utm_campaign=daily%20briefing-oct%2022%202014&utm_medium=email&utm_source=newsletter&ET= bondbuyer%3Ae3226527%3A1048240a%3A&st=email.

[78] See "Non-Rated Municipal Bonds—Understanding the Risks and Opportunities," at http://www.piperjaffray.com/ pdf/02-1624_nonratedmunicipalbonds.pdf.

[79] Compliance with the Volcker Rule would require banks to either hold any securities purchases for more than 60 days or limit their broker-dealer or market-maker activities. A market-maker purchases and maintains an inventory of securities for investor clients. Suppose a bank incorrectly forecasts the future short-term municipal securities demands of its clients.

In this case, demonstrating compliance with the Volcker Rule may depend upon the ability to determine whether the short-term securities trades were made for the benefit the bank (proprietary trading) or its customers (market making). Banks could choose to reduce their inventory of securities (for short-term trades) to minimize risks of non-compliance, thereby reducing the overall liquidity for securities that trade in thin secondary markets. Non-bank institutions may possibly offset the decline in short-term trading by banks, which may help maintain some liquidity in affected securities markets. For more information, See CRS Legal Sidebar WSLG766, What "Proprietary Trading" is Covered by the Volcker Rule?, by M. Maureen Murphy.

[80] See Letter from Alan D. Polsky, Chair, Municipal Securities Rulemaking Board, to Office of the Comptroller of the Currency, Board of Governors of the Federal Reserve System, Federal Deposit Insurance Corporation, Securities and Exchange Commission, January 31, 2012, at http://www.msrb.org/msrb1/Industry-Letters/MSRB-Comment-Letter-onVolcker-Rule.pdf.

[81] See Municipal Securities Rulemaking Board, "MSRB Responds to Adoption of Volcker Rule by Federal Regulators," press release, December 10, 2013, at http://www.msrb.org/News-and-Events/Press-Releases/2013/MSRBResponds-to-Adoption-of-Volcker-Rule-by-Federal-Regulators.aspx.

[82] See Board of Governors of the Federal Reserve System, Commodities Futures Trading Commission, Federal Deposit Insurance Corporation, Office of the Comptroller of the Currency, Securities Exchange Commission, "Agencies Issue Final Rules Implementing the Volcker Rule," press release, December 10, 2013, at http://www.federalreserve.gov/newsevents/press/bcreg/bcreg20131210a3.pdf.

[83] The U.S. Census Bureau estimates that the United States consists of approximately 90,000 municipalities (i.e., states, counties, cities, special tax districts, U.S. territories, such as Washington, DC and Puerto Rico). 83

[84] See CRS Report R41735, State and Local Government Debt: An Analysis, by Steven Maguire. Municipal notes, which may mature within a year or less, may be issued for short-term cash management reasons.

[85] Some private-sector analysts of the municipal bond market analysts have collected more recent proprietary data and report that the gap between revenues and expenditures still has not begun to narrow. See Tom Kozlik and Alan Schankel, "We are Seeing Cracks in the U.S. State Sector and an Unprecedented Multi-Year Run of Credit Deterioration by Some Local Governments," Janney Fixed Income Strategy, Municipal Bond Market Monthly, September 16, 2014, at http://www.janney.com/File%20Library/Fixed%20Income/Janney-MBMM-September2014.pdf.

[86] Estimates regarding the underfunding of pensions range from $1 trillion (see SEC Commissioner Daniel M. Gallagher, "Remarks at Municipal Securities Rulemaking Board's 1st Annual Municipal Securities Regulator Summit," speech, May 29, 2014, at http://www.sec.gov/News/Speech/Detail/Speech/1370541936387) to approximately $4 trillion (see Cory Eucalitto, "Promises Made, Promises Broken-The Betrayal of Pensioners and Taxpayers," State Budget Solutions, September 3, 2013, at http://www.statebudgetsolutions.org/publications/detail/promises-madepromises-broken-the-betrayal-of-pensioners-and-taxpayers).

[87] The reporting treatment of long-term retirement obligations, addressed by the Government Accounting Standards Board, would suggest that numerous public-sector entities have reported these liabilities as supplementary notes that accompany accounting statements rather than reporting them in the financial statements.

[88] The U.S. Census Bureau defines a public-employee pension system as one that is financed by a separate accounting fund (of the administering government), excluding pay-as-you-go insurance plans. See Ceci Villa Ross and Paul Villena, "Annual Survey of Public Pensions: State-Administered Defined Benefit Data Summary Report: 2013," U.S. Census Bureau, August 2014, at http://www2.census.gov/govs/retire/2013_summary_report.pdf.

[89] Municipal localities depend upon the fluctuations in earnings on investments to cover annual pension fund payouts. Some state and local governments issue pension obligation bonds (POBs) to cover pension fund shortfalls. When an investor purchases a POB, the locality uses the proceeds to make its required employee retirement contributions (i.e., defined benefit retirement funds). Ideally, the earnings from high-risk investments (e.g., stocks) would be sufficient enough to cover the anticipated pension fund payouts as well as the initial principal and interest owed to POB investors. See Alicia H. Munnell et al., Pension Obligation Bonds: Financial Crisis Exposes Risks, Center for Retirement Research at Boston College, State and Local Pension Plans, Issue in Brief no. 9, January 2010, at http://crr.bc.edu/wpcontent/uploads/2010/01/SLP_9-508.pdf.

[90] See Georgia's Path2College 529 Plan, "National College Savings Survey Shows Increase in 529 Plan Savings," press release, June 26, 2014, at https://www.path2college 529.com/news/pr-6-26-2014.shtml.

[91] See CRS Report R42807, Tax-Preferred College Savings Plans: An Introduction to 529 Plans, by Margot L. Crandall-Hollick; and Ron Lieber, "College Plans You Thought Were Safe," New York Times, April 1, 2011, at http://www.nytimes.com/2011/04/02/your-money/paying-for-college/02money.html?pagewanted=all&_r=0.

[92] See U.S. Securities and Exchange Commission, "Antion to 529 Plans," at http://www.sec.gov/investor/pubs/ intro529.htm.

[93] Some 529 savings plans are invested in private accounts and are, therefore, unrelated to government budget issues.

[94] See Christina Couch, "College 529 Prepaid Tuition Plans At Risk," Bankrate.com, at http://www.bankrate.com/ finance/college-finance/college-529-prepaid-tuition-plans-at-risk-1.aspx. See Michael A. Olivas, "Developments in 529 Prepaid Tuition Plans (PTP) and College Savings Plans (CSP) Since 2003," University of Houston Law Center, September 2010, at http://www.law.uh.edu/ihelg/monograph/10-05.pdf; and the National Conference of State Legislatures, "Risks of 529 Prepaid Tuition Plans," May 22, 2014, at http://www.ncsl.org/research/education/savingfor-college-529-plans.aspx.

In: U.S. Savings Bonds, Municipal Bonds … ISBN: 978-1-63484-698-1
Editor: Henrietta Walters

Chapter 3

TAX-EXEMPT BONDS: A DESCRIPTION OF STATE AND LOCAL GOVERNMENT DEBT*

Steven Maguire and Jeffrey M. Stupak

SUMMARY

This report provides information about state and local government debt. State and local governments often issue debt instruments in exchange for the use of individuals' and businesses' savings. This debt obligates state and local governments to make interest payments for the use of these savings and to repay, at some time in the future, the amount borrowed. State and local governments finance capital facilities with debt rather than out of current tax revenue in order to match the time pattern of benefits from these capital facilities with the time pattern of tax payments.

The federal government subsidizes the cost of most state and local debt by excluding the interest income from federal income taxation. This tax exemption of interest income is granted because it is believed that state and local capital facilities will be under provided if state and local taxpayers have to pay the full cost. The federal government also provides a tax preference through tax credit bonds (TCBs). With TCBs, the federal government either provides investors with a federal tax credit in lieu of

* This is an edited, reformatted and augmented version of a Congressional Research Service publication RL30638, prepared for Members and Committees of Congress, dated January 9, 2015.

interest payments or a direct payment to the issuer. Qualified Zone Academy Bonds and Build America Bonds are examples.

State and local debt is issued as bonds, to be repaid over a period of time greater than one year and perhaps exceeding 20 years, and as notes, to be repaid within one year. General obligation bonds are secured by the promise to repay with general tax revenue, and revenue bonds are secured with the promise to use the stream of revenue generated by the facility built with the bond proceeds. Most debt is issued to finance new capital facilities, but some is issued to refund a prior bond issue (usually to take advantage of lower interest rates). Tax-exempt bonds issued for some activities are classified as governmental bonds and can be issued without federal constraint because most of the benefits from the capital facilities are enjoyed by the general public. Many tax-exempt revenue bonds are issued for activities Congress has classified as private because most of the benefits from the activities appear to be enjoyed by private individuals and businesses. The annual volume of a subset of these tax-exempt private-activity bonds is capped.

Arbitrage bonds devote a substantial share of the proceeds to the purchase of assets with higher interest rates than that being paid on the tax-exempt bonds. Such arbitrage bonds are not tax exempt because Congress does not want state and local governments to issue tax-exempt bonds and use the proceeds to earn arbitrage profits. The arbitrage profits could substitute for state and local taxes.

One major policy issue in this area is tax reform proposals that would modify the tax treatment of state and local government bonds. Another policy issue is whether constraints should be relaxed on the types of activities, such as infrastructure spending, for which entities can issue tax-exempt debt. The list of activities that classify tax-exempt private-activity bonds—and whether they should be included in the volume cap—is another area of potential change or reform.

WHAT IS DEBT?

Individuals and businesses lend their accumulated savings to borrowers. In exchange, borrowers give lenders a debt instrument. These debt instruments, typically called bonds, represent a promise by borrowers to pay interest income to lenders on the principal (the amount of money borrowed) until the principal is repaid to the lenders. This principal, sometimes called the proceeds, is typically used to finance the construction of capital facilities, but is also used for cash management purposes when revenue collections do not match spending needs during the fiscal year.

WHY DO STATE AND LOCAL GOVERNMENTS ISSUE DEBT?

Since public capital facilities provide services over a long period of time, it makes financial and economic sense to pay for the facilities over a similarly long period of time. This is particularly true for state and local governments. Their taxpayers lay claim to the benefits from these facilities by dint of residency and relinquish their claim to benefits when they move. Given the demands a market-oriented society places on labor mobility, taxpayers are reluctant to pay today for state and local capital services to be received in the future. The rational response of the state or local official concerned with satisfying the preferences of constituents is to match the timing of the payments to the flow of services, precisely the function served by long-term bond financing. An attempt to pay for capital facilities "up front" is likely to result in a less than optimal rate of public capital formation.

State and local governments are also faced with the necessity of planning their budget for the year (or in some cases for two years). This requires a balancing of revenue forecasts against forecasts of the demand for services and spending. Not infrequently, the inevitable unforeseen circumstances that undermine any forecast cause a revenue shortfall, which must be financed with short-term borrowing, or "notes." In addition, even when the forecasts are met, the timing of expenditures may precede the arrival of revenues, creating the necessity to borrow within an otherwise balanced fiscal year. Finally, temporarily high interest rates that prevail at the time bonds are issued to finance a capital project may induce short-term borrowing in anticipation of a drop in rates.

Thus, state and local governments have valid reasons to borrow funds. In fact, these reasons are so universally accepted that both taxpayers and the courts have ignored the 19th century legacy of unrealistically restrictive constitutional and statutory limitations on state and local borrowing.[1]

WHAT MAKES STATE AND LOCAL DEBT SPECIAL?

The federal government has chosen to intervene in the public capital market by granting the debt instruments of state and local governments a unique privilege—the exemption of interest income earned on these bonds from federal income tax. The tax exemption lowers the cost of capital for state and local governments, which should then induce an increase in state and local capital formation. The lower cost of capital arises because investors would be indifferent between taxable bonds (e.g., corporate bonds) that yield a 10% rate of return before taxes and tax-exempt bonds of equivalent risk that yield a 6.5% return. The taxable bond interest earnings carry a tax liability (35% of the interest income in most cases), making the after-tax return on the two bonds identical at 6.5%. Thus, state and local governments could raise capital from investors at an interest cost 3.5 percentage points (350 basis points) lower than a borrower issuing taxable debt.

Generally, the degree to which tax-exempt debt is favored is measured in a variety of ways. Two are fairly common: the yield spread and the yield ratio. The yield spread is the difference between the interest rate on taxable bonds (corporate bonds or U.S. Treasury bonds) and the interest rate on tax-exempt municipal bonds of equivalent risk. *Figure 1* displays the average yield on high-grade tax-exempt bonds and taxable bonds from 1980 to 2013 and the distance between them is the yield spread. Since 1980, the spread between tax-exempt and taxable bonds has declined as underlying interest rates have declined. The greater the yield spread, the greater are the nominal savings to state and local governments as measured by the interest rates they would have to pay if they financed with taxable debt.

Another measure, the yield ratio (which is an average rate on tax-exempt bonds divided by an average rate on a taxable bond of like term and risk), adjusts the spread for the level of interest rates. A lower ratio implies a greater savings to state and local governments relative to taxable debt. As the ratio approaches one, however, tax-exempt borrowing approaches that of taxable borrowing. The ratio was lowest in 1980 and reached a peak in 2012 for Treasury bonds and in 2013 for corporate bonds. Since the financial crisis in 2007, the yield ratio of tax-exempt bonds to Treasury bonds has diverged significantly from the ratio of tax-exempt bonds to corporate bonds. Investors may be signaling that Treasury bonds and corporate bonds are no longer interchangeable investments.

These variations in the cost of state and local borrowing relative to the cost of taxable borrowing arise from changes in the demand for and supply of both tax-exempt and taxable bonds. Demand for tax-exempt bonds depends upon the number of investors, their wealth, statutory tax rates, and alternative investment opportunities. Supply depends upon the desire of the state and local sector for capital facilities and their ability to engage in conduit financing (issuing state or local government bonds and passing the proceeds through to businesses or individuals for their private use). Almost all of the factors which influence demand and supply are affected by federal tax policy and fiscal policy.

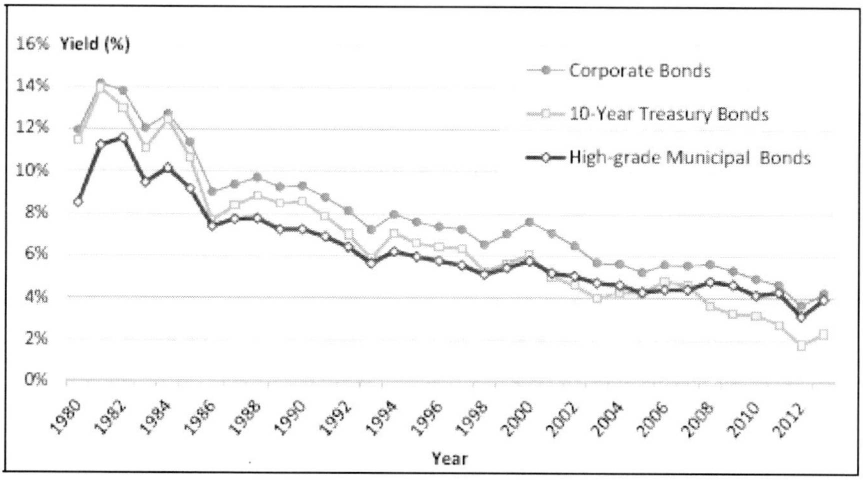

Source: Council of Economic Advisors, Economic Report of the President, February 2014, Table B-17.

Figure 1. Tax-Exempt and Taxable Bonds: Yield Spread and Yield Ratio, 1980 to 2013.

Another measure, the yield ratio (which is an average rate on tax-exempt bonds divided by an average rate on a taxable bond of like term and risk), adjusts the spread for the level of interest rates. A lower ratio implies a greater savings to state and local governments relative to taxable debt. As the ratio approaches one, however, tax-exempt borrowing approaches that of taxable borrowing. The ratio was lowest in 1980 and reached a peak in 2012 for Treasury bonds and in 2013 for corporate bonds. Since the financial crisis in 2007, the yield ratio of tax-exempt bonds to Treasury bonds has diverged significantly from the ratio of tax-exempt bonds to corporate bonds. Investors may be signaling that Treasury bonds and corporate bonds are no longer interchangeable investments.

These variations in the cost of state and local borrowing relative to the cost of taxable borrowing arise from changes in the demand for and supply of both tax-exempt and taxable bonds. Demand for tax-exempt bonds depends upon the number of investors, their wealth, statutory tax rates, and alternative investment opportunities. Supply depends upon the desire of the state and local sector for capital facilities and their ability to engage in conduit financing (issuing state or local government bonds and passing the proceeds through to businesses or individuals for their private use). Almost all of the factors which influence demand and supply are affected by federal tax policy and fiscal policy.

WHAT DOES TAX EXEMPTION COST THE FEDERAL GOVERNMENT?

The direct cost to the federal government of this interest exclusion is the individual and corporate income tax revenue forgone. Consider a 35% marginal tax rate corporate investor who purchases a 6.5% tax-exempt bond with principal of $1,000 that is to be repaid after 20 years. Each year for 20 years this taxpayer receives $65 in tax-exempt interest income. Each year the federal government forgoes collecting $35 of revenue because the revenue loss is based upon the yield the taxpayer forgoes. For example, if the investor had purchased a taxable bond carrying a 10% interest rate, he would have received $100 in interest income and paid $35 in income taxes on that income.[2]

The annual federal revenue loss (or tax expenditure) on the outstanding stock of tax-exempt bonds issued for public purposes is reported in the *Analytical Perspectives* section of the Budget every year. The estimates for the last 20 years are displayed in *Table 1*.[3] Because they are based upon the outstanding stock of public-purpose tax-exempt bonds, it takes time for some legislative changes to show up in these data. The amount of forgone tax revenue from the exclusion of interest income on public-purpose tax-exempt bonds is substantial, $28.4 billion in 2013. Over the 2015 to 2019 budget window, the estimated loss of revenue is expected to be $213.8 billion, or the 12th-largest tax expenditure.[4]

WHY DOES THE FEDERAL GOVERNMENT SUBSIDIZE STATE AND LOCAL DEBT?

When first introduced in 1913, the federal income tax excluded the interest income earned by holders of the debt obligations of states and their political subdivisions from taxable income. It was asserted by many that any taxation of this interest income would be unconstitutional because the exemption was protected by the Tenth Amendment and the doctrine of intergovernmental tax immunity. The U.S. Supreme Court rejected this claim of constitutional protection in 1988 in *South Carolina v. Baker* (485 U.S. 505, [1988]).

Table 1. Tax Expenditure on the Outstanding Stock of Public Purpose Tax-Exempt Bonds: 1994 to 2013

(in billions)

Year	Tax Expenditure	Year	Tax Expenditure
1994	$19.6	2004	$26.2
1995	$20.4	2005	$26.4
1996	$24.9	2006	$23.0
1997	$19.9	2007	$23.5
1998	$24.6	2008	$24.6
1999	$27.5	2009	$23.0
2000	$26.8	2010	$30.4
2001	$27.4	2011	$26.2
2002	$29.9	2012	$26.0
2003	$31.1	2013	$28.4

Source: Office of Management and Budget. Analytical Perspectives: Budget of the United States Government, Table 14-1 (in budget for FY2015), various years.

Although the legal basis for the subsidy is statutory rather than constitutional, the policy reason for the subsidy is economic. Economic theory suggests that certain types of goods and services will not be provided in the correct or "optimal" amounts by the private sector because some of the benefits are consumed collectively, a street light for example. The nation's welfare can be increased by public provision of these goods and services, and some of these public goods and services are best provided by state or local governments. Some of the goods and services provided by state or local governments, however, benefit both residents, who pay local taxes, and nonresidents, who pay minimal if any local taxes. Since state and local taxpayers are likely to be unwilling to provide these services to nonresidents without compensation, it is probable that state and local services will be under provided. In theory, the cost reduction provided by the exemption of interest income compensates state and local taxpayers for benefits provided to nonresidents. This encourages the governments to provide the optimal amount of public services.

CLASSIFYING STATE AND LOCAL DEBT INSTRUMENTS

State and local debt can be classified based on (1) the *maturity* (or term), which is the length of time before the principal is repaid; (2) the *type of security*, which is the financial backing for the debt; (3) the *use of the proceeds* for either new facilities or to refinance previously issued bonds; and (4) whether the *type of activity* being financed has a public or a private purpose. Another important factor is the level of risk. Just about every bond issued by a state or local government is rated based on the probability of default. The privately managed rating agencies incorporate all of the above factors as well as the financial health of the entity issuing the bonds when arriving upon a bond rating. The higher the default risk, the lower the rating.

Maturity: Short-Term vs. Long-Term

Tax and Revenue Anticipation Notes

State and local governments must borrow money for long periods of time and for short periods of time. Long-term debt instruments are usually referred to as bonds, and carry maturities in excess of one year. Short-term debt instruments are usually referred to as notes, and carry maturities of 12 months or less. If the notes are to be paid from specific taxes due in the near future, they usually are called tax anticipation notes (TANs); if from anticipated intergovernmental revenue, they are called revenue anticipation notes (RANs). If the notes are to be paid from long-term borrowing (e.g., bonds), they are called bond anticipation notes (BANs). Tax anticipation notes and revenue anticipation notes are often grouped together and referred to as tax and revenue anticipation notes (TRANs). *Figure 2* displays the volume of long-term and short-term borrowing since 1992. Long-term borrowing dominates state and local debt activity in most years, with the long-term share peaking in 2006 at 89.8% of this market.

Auction Rate Securities

Auction Rate Securities (ARSs) are long-term debt obligations with the unique feature of adjustable or variable interest rates.[5] In contrast to long-term, fixed rate securities, issuers go to auction periodically (anywhere from every 7 to 35 days) to reset the interest rate on the debt outstanding.

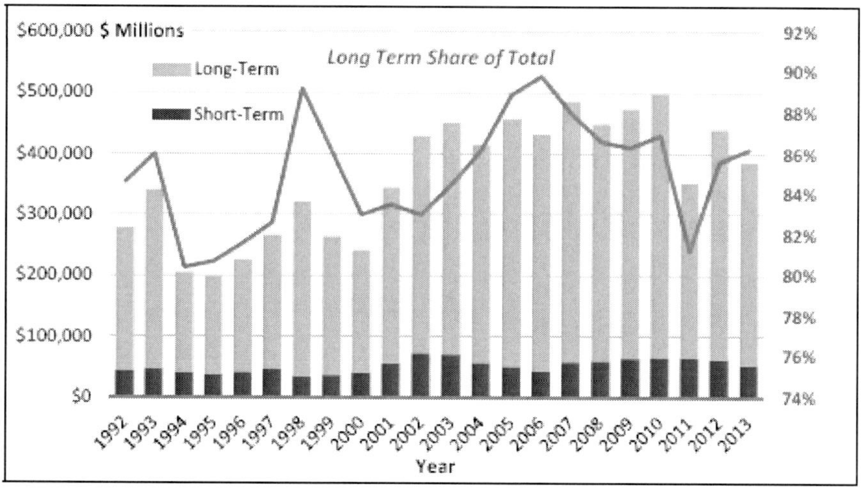

Source: The Bond Buyer Yearbook, 2014.

Figure 2. Volume of State and Local Government Debt.

The auction mechanism and interest rate parameters vary by issuer (and issue) though most use what is termed a "Dutch auction" where each bidder submits a bid for the amount they are willing to purchase at a given interest rate. All bids are ordered from lowest interest rate to highest interest rate and the rate where the market clears, that is, where all bonds would be purchased, establishes the new ARS rate. All bidders receive that rate.

Unique Features of ARSs

ARSs typically have a "call option" where the issuer can buy the ARS back at par (face value) at any scheduled auction and then retire the debt. Most ARSs are insured by the issuer because they *do not* carry a "put" option that would allow bondholders to sell the bonds at a specified price to the issuer or a designated third party. The bond insurance reduces risk and thus interest rate, making the bonds less costly to issuers. For this reason, ARSs are

very sensitive to changes in credit ratings and normally require the highest ratings (e.g., AAA/Aaa) to make them marketable. This is usually achieved with bond insurance.[6]

A Failed Auction

The existing holders of ARSs offer bids as well as new bidders. If all bids of both existing bond reservation rate is typically significantly higher than current market interest rates. Because the rate is higher than market interest rates, issuers of ARSs wish to avoid paying the reservation rate.

Growth and Decline of ARSs

The issuance of ARSs grew considerably from 1988 through 2007. In 1988, the Bond Buyer identified one ARS issue valued at $25 million; none were issued in 1987.[7] In 2004, the peak year, 438 ARS bonds valued at $42.5 billion were issued. No ARSs have been issued since 2007, roughly corresponding to the beginning of the financial crisis, when 322 were sold for a total value of $38.7 billion.

Security: General Obligation, Revenue, and Lease Rental Bonds

Another important characteristic of tax-exempt bonds is the security provided to the bondholder. General obligation (GO) bonds pledge the full faith and credit of the issuing government. The issuing government makes an unconditional pledge to use its powers of taxation to honor its liability for interest and principal repayment. Revenue bonds, or non-guaranteed debt, pledge only the earnings from revenue-producing activities, most often the earnings from the facilities being financed with the revenue bonds. Should these earnings prove to be inadequate to honor these commitments, the issuing government is under no obligation to use its taxing powers to finance the shortfall. Some revenue bonds are issued with credit enhancements provided by insurance or bank letters of credit that guarantee payment upon such a revenue shortfall.

Figure 3 displays the breakdown between long-term GO and revenue bonds since 1992. The long-term market has been and continues to be dominated by revenue bonds, which are nonguaranteed debt instruments. The revenue bond share has fluctuated between 61% and 72% from 1992 through 2013.

All tax-exempt interest income attributable to state and local governments does not appear in the form of bonds. Governments may engage in installment purchase contracts and finance leases for which the portion of the installment or lease payment to a vendor is tax exempt. For example, computer equipment or road building equipment could be leased from a vendor using a rental agreement or an installment sales contract. Under this type of agreement, the monthly payments to the vendor are large enough to cover the vendor's interest expense on the funds borrowed to purchase the equipment which was leased to the government. This portion that is attributable to interest income is not included in the vendor's taxable income. Such transactions are often referred to as municipal leasing.

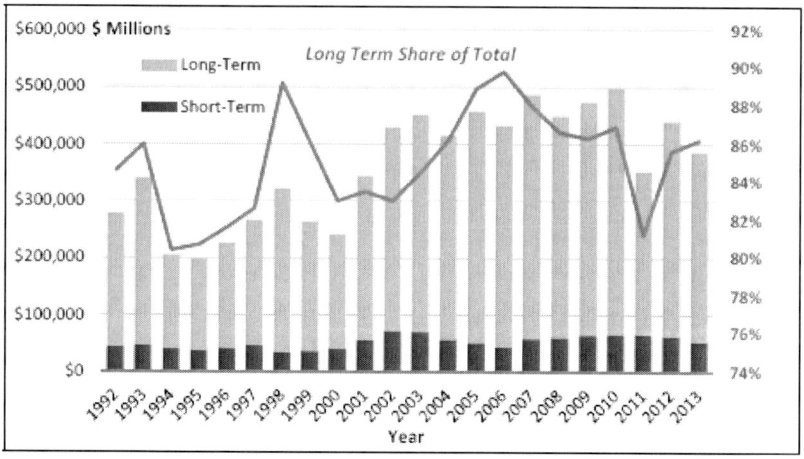

Source: The Bond Buyer Yearbook, 2014.

Figure 3. Volume of Long-Term Tax-Exempt Debt: General Obligation (GO) and Revenue Bonds, 1992 to 2013.

Lease rental revenue bonds and certificates are variations on revenue bonds. An authority or nonprofit corporation issues bonds, builds a facility with the proceeds, and leases the facility to a municipality. Security for the bonds or certificates is based on the lease payments. When the bonds are retired, the facility belongs to the lessee (the municipality). An advantage to this type of arrangement is that many states' constitutional and statutory definitions do not consider this type of financing to be debt because the lease payments are annual operating expenses based upon appropriated monies.

The leasing technique has also been used to provide tax-exempt funds to nonprofit organizations. A municipality issues the bonds for the construction of a facility that is leased to a nonprofit hospital or university. Again, security for the bonds is based on the lease payments.

Use of the Proceeds: New-Issue vs. Refunding Bonds

Long-term tax-exempt bond issues also can be characterized by their status as new issues or refunding issues. New issues represent bonds issued to finance new capital facilities. Refundings usually are made to replace outstanding bonds with bonds that carry lower interest rates or other favorable terms. As such, the refunding bonds usually do not add to the stock of outstanding bonds or the capital stock. The proceeds of the refunding bonds are used to pay off the remaining principal of the original bond issue, which is retired. Advance refunding bonds, however, do add to the outstanding stock of bonds without adding to the stock of capital. Advance refunding bonds are issued prior to the date on which the original bonds are refunded, so that for a period of time there are two bond issues outstanding to finance the same capital facilities.

The volume of refunding shares varies widely, depending to a great extent on changes in the relative magnitudes of taxable and tax-exempt interest rates. Note that the 1993 increase in the top marginal individual income tax rates may have increased the demand for tax-exempt bonds. Higher tax rates make tax-exempt bonds more attractive relative to taxable bonds, all other things being equal. The increased demand and accompanying lower interest rates may have prompted state and local governments to replace outstanding issues with refunding bonds that carried lower interest rates. In contrast, refundings dropped considerably in 1999 and 2000. The decline could have been in response to higher interest rates or to strong economic conditions in most states which minimized the need for debt finance generally. The story is reversed from 2001 to 2003 as the economy slowed and state budgets were strained by lower tax revenue collections. New issues in 2003 were more than double the amount of new issues in 2000. In 2005, GO bonds and refunding bond volume peaked, likely reflecting the historically low interest rates on tax-exempt debt. The low rate environment since 2011 has also pushed up the share of refunding issues.

Public Purpose vs. Private Purpose

An important characteristic of tax-exempt bonds is the purpose or activity for which the bonds are issued. Most of the tax legislation pertaining to tax-exempt bonds over the last 30 years reflects an effort to restrict tax exemption to bonds issued for activities that satisfy some broadly defined "public" purpose, that is, for which federal taxpayers are likely to receive substantial benefits. Bonds are considered to be for a public purpose if they satisfy either of two criteria: less than 10% of the proceeds are used directly or indirectly by a non-governmental entity; or less than 10% of the bond proceeds are secured directly or indirectly by property used in a trade or business. Bonds that satisfy either of these tests are termed "governmental" bonds and can be issued without federal limit. Bonds that fail both of these tests are termed "private-activity" bonds (PABs) because they provide significant benefits to private individuals or businesses. These projects are ineligible for tax-exempt financing.

Activities which fail the two tests but are considered to provide both public and private benefits have been termed eligible or *qualified* PABs. These selected activities can be financed with tax-exempt bonds. *Table 2* provides the dollar value of new issues of tax-exempt private-activity bonds and their share of total private-activity volume capacity for 2012 and 2013. *Figure 4* provides historical data on the portion of PAB volume to total bond volume.

Table 2. Private-Activity Bond Volume by Type of Activity in 2012 and 2013

	Allocation in Billions		*Percent of Capacity Available*	
Capacity Allocation	*2012*	*2013*	*2012*	*2013*
Total Volume Capacity Available	*$79,295.00*	*$87,223.50*	*100.00%*	*100.00%*
New Volume Capacity	$32,469.10	$32,748.30	40.95%	37.55%
Carry Forward from Previous Years	$50,611.10	$56,445.30	63.83%	64.71%
Total Carryforward to Next Year	*$46,678.70*	*$60,220.00*	*58.87%*	*69.04%*
Total PABs Issued	*$11,088.80*	*$8,824.30*	*13.98%*	*10.12%*
Single-family Mortgage Revenue	$2,654.40	$1,828.20	3.35%	2.10%
Multi-family Housinga	$5,003.90	$4,722.30	6.31%	5.41%
Mortgage Credit Certificates	$2,564.70	$3,441.20	3.23%	3.95%
Exempt Facilities	$7,391.30	$6,076.00	9.32%	6.97%
Other Activities	$30.10	$84.20	0.04%	0.10%
Student Loans	$772.00	$480.20	0.97%	0.55%
Industrial Development	$240.40	$355.80	0.30%	0.41%
Abandon Capacity	$6,604.80	$11,751.60	8.33%	13.47%

Source: "CDFA's 2013 Annual Volume Cap Report," July 2014; and "CDFA's 2012 Annual Volume Cap Data," July 2014. The data are available at http://www.cdfa.net/.

[a] Multifamily housing bonds are an allowable use of exempt facility bonds and are also included in the "Exempt Facility" category.

Private Activities Eligible for Tax Exemption

All tax-exempt private-activity bonds are subject to restrictions that do not apply to governmental bonds, chief among them being no advance refundings and the inclusion of the interest income in the alternative minimum income tax base. In addition, the annual dollar value of all bonds issued for most of these activities by all governmental units within a state is limited to the greater of $100 per resident or $348.91 million in 2014.

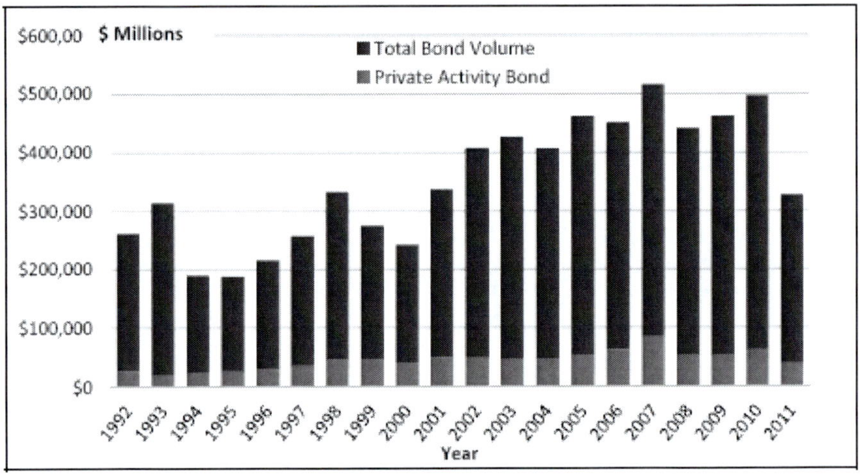

Source: The 1992 to 1995 data are from Nutter, Sarah, "Tax-Exempt Private Activity Bonds, 1988-1995," SOI Bulletin, Summer 1999; Belmonte, Cynthia, "Tax-Exempt Bonds, 2003-2004," SOI Bulletin, Fall 2006; Belmonte, Cynthia, "Tax-Exempt Bonds, 2005," SOI Bulletin, Fall 2007; and for later years the IRS data are available at http://www.irs.ustreas.gov/taxstats/charitablestats/article/0,,id=97029,00.html. Total long-term bond volume data are from the Bond Buyer Yearbook 2014.

Figure 4. New-Money and Long-Term Private-Activity Bond Volume, 1992 to 2011.

The cap has been adjusted for inflation since 2004. The annual volume cap applies to the total of bonds issued primarily for but not limited to multi- and single-family housing, industrial development, exempt facilities,[8] student loans, and bond-financed takeovers of investor-owned utilities (usually electric utilities).

Bonds issued for several activities classified as private are not subject to the volume cap if the facilities are governmentally owned.[9] These activities are airports, docks, and wharves; nonprofit organization facilities; high-speed inter-urban rail facilities; and solid waste disposal facilities that produce electric energy. *Table 3* below reports the estimated tax expenditure for selected private activities that qualify for financing with tax-exempt debt.

Recently, Congress has further expanded the types of private activities eligible for tax-exempt financing and has increased the capacity for selected activities and issuers. A brief description of legislation that Congress has enacted since 2001 follows below.

Table 3. Federal Tax Expenditure for Selected Private Activities Financed with Tax-Exempt Bonds

Private Activity	2013 Tax Expenditure (in millions)	Percentage of Total
Total of Selected Activities	*$10,020*	*100.00%*
Energy Facilities	$20	0.20%
Water, Sewerage, and Hazardous Waste Disposal	$450	4.49%
Small-Issues	$170	1.70%
Owner-Occupied Mortgage Subsidy	$1,230	12.28%
Rental Housing	$1,000	9.98%
Airports, Docks, and Similar Facilities	$740	7.39%
Student Loans	$510	5.09%
Private Nonprofit Educational Facilities	$2,240	22.36%
Hospital Construction	$3,430	34.23%
Veterans' Housing	$10	0.10%
GO Zone and GO Zone Mortgage	$220	2.20%

Source: Office of Management and Budget. Analytical Perspectives: Budget of the United States Government, Fiscal Year 2015, Table 14-1, pp. 205-209.

Economic Growth and Tax Relief Reconciliation Act of 2001

As part of the Economic Growth and Tax Relief Reconciliation Act of 2001 (P.L. 107-16), a new type of tax-exempt private-activity bond was created beginning on January 1, 2002.[10] The act expanded the definition of "an exempt facility bond" to include bonds issued for qualified public educational facilities. Bonds issued for qualified educational facilities are not counted against a state's private-activity volume cap. However, the qualified public educational facility bonds have their own volume capacity limit equal to the greater of $10 multiplied by the state population or $5 million. Since nearly all states would be better off with the $10 per capita limit, the potential new debt would have been approximately $2.8 billion in 2001 if the bonds were available in 2001.

Job Creation and Worker Assistance Act of 2002

The JCWA 2002 (P.L. 107-147) created the New York Liberty Zone (NYLZ) in the wake of the September 11, 2001, terrorist attacks. The legislation included several tax benefits for the NYLZ intended to foster economic revitalization within the NYLZ. Specifically, the so-called "Liberty Bond" program allows New York State (in conjunction and coordination with New York City) to issue up to $8 billion of tax-exempt private-activity bonds for qualified facilities in the NYLZ. Qualified facilities follow the exempt facility rules within Section 142 of the IRC. The original deadline to issue the bonds was January 1, 2005, but was extended to January 1, 2014, by the American Taxpayer Relief Act (P.L. 112-240).

American Jobs Creation Act

In 2004, the American Jobs Creation Act (P.L. 108-357) created bonds for "qualified green building and sustainable design projects." The bonds are exempt from the state volume cap and are instead limited to an aggregate of $2 billion for bonds issued between January 1, 2005, and October 1, 2009.

The Safe, Accountable, Flexible, Efficient, Transportation Equity Act of 2005

This legislation created a new type of tax-exempt private activity bond for the construction of rail to highway (or highway to rail) transfer facilities. The national limit is $15 billion and the bonds are not subject to state volume caps for private activity bonds. The Secretary of Transportation allocates the bond authority on a project-by-project basis.

Gulf Opportunity Zone Act of 2005

The hurricanes that struck the Gulf region in late summer 2005 prompted Congress to create a tax-advantaged economic development zone intended to encourage investment and rebuilding in the Gulf region. The Gulf Opportunity Zone (GOZ) was comprised of the counties where the Federal Emergency Management Agency (FEMA) declared the inhabitants to be eligible for individual and public assistance. Based on proportion of state personal income, the Katrina-affected portion of the GOZ represents approximately 73% of Louisiana's economy, 69% of Mississippi's, and 18% of Alabama's.

Specifically, the "Gulf Opportunity Zone Act of 2005" (GOZA 2005, P.L. 109-135) contained two provisions that expanded the amount of private-activity bonds outstanding and language to relax the eligibility rules for mortgage revenue bonds. The most significant is the provision that increased the volume cap for private-activity bonds issued for Hurricane Katrina recovery in Alabama, Louisiana, and Mississippi (identified as the Gulf Opportunity Zone, or "GO Zone"). GOZA 2005 added $2,500 per person in the federally declared Katrina disaster areas in which the residents qualified for individual and public assistance.

The increased volume capacity added approximately $2.2 billion for Alabama, $7.8 billion for Louisiana, and $4.8 billion for Mississippi in aggregate over five years. The legislation defined "qualified project costs" that are eligible for bond financing as (1) the cost of any qualified residential rental project (26 §142(d)); and (2) the cost of acquisition, construction, reconstruction, and renovation of—(i) nonresidential real property (including fixed improvements associated with such property) and (ii) public utility property (26 §168(i)(10)), in the GOZ. The additional capacity was to have to been issued before January 1, 2011.

The second provision allowed for advance refunding of certain tax-exempt bonds. Under GOZA 2005, governmental bonds issued by Alabama, Louisiana, and Mississippi could be advance refunded an additional time and exempt facility private-activity bonds for airports, docks, and wharves once. Private-activity bonds are otherwise not eligible for advance refunding (see earlier discussion of advance refunding).

The Housing and Economic Recovery Act of 2008

In response to the housing crisis of 2008, Congress included two provisions in the Housing and Economic Recovery Act of 2008 (HERA; P.L. 110-289) that were intended to assist the housing sector. First, HERA provided that interest on qualified private activity bonds issued for (1) qualified residential rental projects, (2) qualified mortgage bonds, and (3) qualified veterans' mortgage bonds would not be subject to the AMT. In addition, HERA also created an additional $11 billion of volume cap space for bonds issued for qualified mortgage bonds and qualified bonds for residential rental projects. The cap space was designated for 2008 but could have been carried forward through 2010.

The American Recovery and Reinvestment Act of 2009

In response to the financial crisis and economic recession, Congress included several bond-related provisions in the American Recovery and Reinvestment Act of 2009 (ARRA; P.L. 111-5). The following three provisions were intended to make bond finance less expensive for the designated projects. One expanded the definition of qualified manufacturing facilities (under §144(a)(12)(C)) to include the creation and production of intangible property including patents, copyrights, formulae, etc. Before ARRA, only tangible property was eligible. The second created a new category of private activity bond called "recovery zone facility bonds." The bonds were to be used for investment in infrastructure, job training, education, and economic development in economically distressed areas. The bonds, which were subject to a separate national cap of $15 billion were allocated to the states based on the decline in employment in 2008. The bonds were to be issued in 2009 and 2010.

A third provision provided $2 billion for tribal governments to issue tax-exempt bonds for economic development purposes. The tax code currently allows tribal governments to issue debt for "essential government services" only. Many economic development projects would not qualify absent this ARRA provision.

WHAT ARE ARBITRAGE BONDS?

Many individuals and businesses make money by engaging in arbitrage, borrowing money at one interest rate and lending that borrowed money to others at a higher interest rate. The difference between the rate at which one borrows and the rate at which one lends produces arbitrage earnings. At its most basic level, it is the primary activity of commercial banks—pay depositors an interest rate of "x" and use the deposits to make commercial, automobile, and home loans at "x + y" interest rate. In this context, arbitrage is a time-honored and appropriate financial market activity.

That is not the case in the tax-exempt bond market. State and local governments do not pay federal income tax, and absent federal constraint, have unlimited capacity to issue debt at low interest rates and reinvest the bond proceeds in higher-yielding taxable debt instruments, thereby earning arbitrage profits. Unchecked, state and local governments could substitute arbitrage earnings for a substantial portion of their own citizens' tax effort.

Congress has decided that such arbitrage should be limited, and that tax-exempt bond proceeds must be used as quickly as possible to pay contractors for the construction of the capital facilities for which the bonds were issued. Since it is impossible for bonds to be issued precisely when contractors must be paid for their expenses incurred in building public capital facilities, the tax law provides a three-year period to spend an increasing share of the bond proceeds. Bond issues that have unspent proceeds in excess of the allowed amounts during this three-year spend-down schedule must rebate any arbitrage earnings to the Department of the Treasury. Bond issues are considered to be taxable arbitrage bonds if a governmental unit, in violation of the arbitrage restriction in the tax code, invested a substantial portion of the proceeds "to acquire higher yielding investments, or to replace funds which were used directly or indirectly to acquire higher yielding investments."[11]

WHAT ARE TAX CREDIT BONDS?

Tax Credit Bonds (TCBs) are a type of bond that offers an investor a federal tax credit or the issuer a direct payment. Build America Bonds (BABs), which are no longer issued, are a type of TCB that offers a direct payment to the issuer.

There are a variety of other TCBs in addition to BABs. Qualified zone academy bonds (QZABs), which were the first tax credit bonds, were introduced as part of the Taxpayer Relief Act of 1997 (P.L. 105-34) and were first issued in 1998. Clean renewable energy bonds (CREBs) were created by the Energy Policy Act of 2005 (P.L. 109-58) and "new" CREBs by the Emergency Economic Stabilization Act of 2008 (P.L. 110-343). Gulf tax credit bonds (GTCBs) were created by the Gulf Opportunity Zone Act of 2005 (P.L. 109-135), but authority to issue GTCBs has expired. Qualified forestry conservation bonds (QFCBs) were created by the Food, Conservation, and Energy Act of 2008 (P.L. 110-246). Qualified energy conservation bonds (QECBs) and Midwest Disaster Bonds (MWDBs) were created by the Emergency Economic Stabilization Act of 2008 (P.L. 110-343).

The American Recovery and Reinvestment Act of 2009 (P.L. 111-5, ARRA) included several bond provisions that use a tax credit or issue direct payment. Specifically, ARRA created Qualified School Constructions Bonds (QSCBs), BABs, and Recovery Zone Economic Development Bonds (RZEDBs). Unlike other tax credit bonds, the interest rate on the BABs and RZEDBs is a rate agreed to by the issuer and investor and the issuers receive direct payments from the Treasury. In contrast, the Secretary of the Treasury sets the credit rate for the other TCBs. The authority to issue BABs and RZEDBs expired after 2010.

Each TCB, with the exception of BABs, is designated for a specific purpose, location, or project. Issuers use the proceeds for public school construction and renovation; clean renewable energy projects; refinancing of outstanding government debt in regions affected by natural disasters;

conservation of forest land; investment in energy conservation; and for economic development purposes. All of the TCBs are temporary tax provisions.

The QZAB and QSCB credit rate is set at 100% and the "new CREB" and QECB credit rate is set at 70% of the interest cost. In contrast, the BAB tax credit rate is 35%. QZABs are typically extended as part of so-called "extenders" legislation. They expired after 2013 but were retroactively extended through 2014 by the Tax Increase Prevention Act of 2014 (P.L. 113-295).

Legislative Issues

Current legislative interest focuses on altering the tax treatment of state and local debt to provide a more economically efficient subsidy with a lower federal revenue cost.[12] There are three primary types of proposals that include changes to state and local government bonds—capping the preference, eliminating the preference, and changing the preference to a direct issuer subsidy. These three types can be seen in the following proposals. The President's FY2015 budget proposal would include partial elimination of the tax preference by capping the preference at the 28% marginal tax rate. The Simpson-Bowles (SB) deficit reduction plan proposes complete elimination of the tax preference.[13] The Congressional Budget Office (CBO) "Revenue Options" report proposes eliminating the tax exemption for new qualified private activity bonds which would generate a budget savings of $30 billion over the 2015 to 2024 budget window.[14] The direction of broader tax reform will likely dictate which modifications, if any, are made to the tax treatment of state and local government debt.

Suggested Readings

Hilhouse, Albert M. *Municipal Bonds: A Century of Experience* (New York: Prentice-Hall, 1936).

The classic history of the use and development of municipal bonds from their introduction in the 19th century.

U.S. Senate. Committee on the Budget. *Tax Expenditures: Compendium of Background Material on Individual Provisions.* S.Prt. 112-45. 112th Congress, 2nd session, December 2012.

Provides description, revenue loss estimate, and economic analysis of the effects of governmental bonds and each major category of private-activity bond.

Zimmerman, Dennis. *The Private Use of Tax-Exempt Bonds: Controlling Public Subsidy of Private Activity* (Washington: The Urban Institute Press, 1991).

Provides institutional background: history, legal framework, and industry characteristics. Provides discussion of tax-exempt bonds as an economic policy tool affecting: intergovernmental fiscal relations, the federal budget deficit, efficient resource allocation, and tax equity. Provides a history and economic analysis of tax-exempt bond legislation from 1968 to 1989.

End Notes

[1] Dennis Zimmerman, "History of Municipal Bonds," in his *The Private Use of Tax-Exempt Bonds: Controlling the Public Subsidy of Private Activity* (Washington, The Urban Institute Press, 1991), pp. 17-27.

[2] The decision about preferred alternatives is critical to estimates of the revenue loss from tax-exempt bonds. An entire range of financial and real assets exists with different yields, risk, and degree of preferential taxation. It is not true that the municipal bond purchaser's preferred alternative is always a taxable bond.

[3] These estimates are derived by summing the revenue loss estimates for each activity listed in the tax expenditures budget. Technically, this is incorrect because each activity's revenue loss is calculated in isolation, and there are interactive effects. Nonetheless, without an estimate of the interactive effects' impact on revenue loss, the summing employed here provides the best available order of magnitude.

[4] Office of Management and Budget. *Analytical Perspectives: FY2015 Budget of the United States Government*, Table 14-3.

[5] For more see CRS Report RL34672, *Auction-Rate Securities*, by D. Andrew Austin.

[6] Douglas Skarr, California Debt and Investment Advisory Commission, "Auction Rate Securities," *Issue Brief*, Aug. 2004, pp. 2-3.

[7] *The Bond Buyer 2007 Yearbook*, SourceMedia Inc., New York, NY.

[8] Exempt facilities subject to the volume cap are the following: mass commuting facilities, water furnishing, sewage treatment, solid waste disposal, residential rental projects, electric energy or gas furnishing, local district heating or cooling provision, and hazardous waste disposal and 25% of high-speed rail facility bonds. 26 I.R.C. §141(e), §142(a), and §146(g).

[9] This does not mean governmental ownership in the conventional sense. It simply means that lease arrangements for private management and operation of bond-financed facilities must be structured to deny accelerated depreciation benefits to the private operator, lease length

must conform to the facility's expected service life, and any sale of the facility to the private operator must be made at fair market value. 26 I.R.C. §146(g).

[10] For a more extensive explanation of the tax exempt bond provisions in EGTRRA, see CRS Report RS20932, *Tax-Exempt Bond Provisions in the "Economic Growth and Tax Relief Reconciliation Act of 2001"*, by Steven Maguire.

[11] 26 I.R.C. §148(a).

[12] For more, see CRS Report R42396, *The Impact of Budget Proposals on Tax-Exempt Bonds*, by Steven Maguire.

[13] The White House, The National Commission on Fiscal Responsibility and Reform, The Moment of Truth, December 2010, available at http://www.fiscalcommission.gov/sites/ fiscalcommission.gov/files/documents/ TheMomentofTruth12_1_2010.pdf.

[14] Congressional Budget Office, "Options for Reducing the Deficit: 2015 to 2024," November 2014, p. 134. Available at http://www.cbo.gov/budget-options/2014.

INDEX

F

G

M

N

O

P